Baking

with friends

# Baking
## with friends

# Recipes, Tips and Fun Facts
# for Teaching Kids to Bake

By
**Sharon Davis and Charlene Patton**

Illustrations by
**Coleen McIntyre**

Edited by
**Nicholas Beatty**

Goops Unlimited
- A Family Academy Book -
P.O. Box 1840
Battle Ground, Washington 98604

www.TheGoops.com

Baking with Friends:
Recipes, Tips, and Fun Facts for Teaching Kids to Bake
Goops Unlimited  c. 2010

By Sharon Davis and Charlene Patton
Home Baking Association, www.homebaking.org

Original Watercolors Illustrations by Coleen McIntyre

Nutrition Analysis by Jana Patton, Clinical Dietician

Edited by Nicholas Beatty

Design by Liz Eisenbraun and Stephanie Eisenbraun

Printed In Korea

Publisher's Cataloging-In-Publication Data
(Prepared by The Donohue Group, Inc.)

Baking with friends : recipes, tips, and fun facts for teaching kids to bake / edited by Nicholas Beatty ;
by Charlene Patton & Sharon Davis ; illustrations by Coleen McIntyre.

p. : col. ill. ;  cm. + 1 sound disc.

Accompanying CD includes additional content read by Pam Atherton.
Summary: Baking recipes for families, with an emphasis on child involvement.

Includes educational materials for teachers, parents, and youth mentors.
Interest age level: 006-012.
ISBN-13: 978-0-9712368-2-0
ISBN-10: 0-9712368-2-8

1. Cookery--Juvenile literature.  2. Baking--Juvenile literature.  3. Cookery.  4. Baking.  I. Beatty, Nicholas.
II. Patton, Charlene.  III. Davis, Sharon P.  IV. McIntyre, Coleen.

TX652.5 .B35 2010

641.5123                                                                                    2009941195

# Baking with friends

## Introduction

From brownies to yeast breads, baking provides opportunities to teach kitchen skills and explore the science and wonder of mixing ingredients. There are many opportunities to share the joy of baking in the home kitchen, school, or community center, thus making a difference in the lives of children.

The Home Baking Association has been dedicated to developing resources to help teach baking for more than fifty years. In their latest contribution, *Baking with Friends*, each recipe includes a family baking activity, vocabulary word, and fun fact to enhance the baking experience. In addition, a compilation of helpful resources at the end of the book further develop educational opportunities for children learning to bake.

Baking with Friends would not be possible without the generous support of Mary Sue Peterson, Test Kitchen Manager; Land O'Lakes, Brenda Alten, Director of Public Relations, The J.M. Smucker Company; and Jana Patton, Clinical Dietitian, Cotton-O'Neil Heart Center.

# Contents:

## Cookies and Bars
6 Designer Oatmeal Cookies
8 Forgotten Chocolate
   Chip Cookies
10 Fudge Brownies

## Desserts
12 Apple Dumplings
   in Cinnamon Sauce
14 Country Fruit Cobbler
16 Gingerbread
18 Hot Fudge Pudding Cake
20 Lazy Daisy Cake
22 Old-Fashioned
   Apple Cake Dessert
24 Quilt Patch Cake
26 Rustic Country Fruit Tart

## Quick Breads
28 Confetti Cornbread
30 Crispy Whole Grain Waffles
32 Flour Tortillas
34 Katy's A+ Crepes
36 Pumpkin Pancakes

## Main Dishes
38 Basic Whole Wheat Pizza
40 Chicken and Dumpling Soup
42 Cheese Quesadillas

## Yeast Breads and Rolls
44 100% Whole Wheat Bread
46 Bread Sticks
48 Easy 1, 2, 3 Soft Pretzels
50 Fruited Focaccia
52 Grandma's Refrigerator Dough
54 Monkey Bread
56 Cinnamon Rolls
58 Pilgrim Bread
60 Pita Pocket Bread

## Miscellaneous
62 Great Grains Granola
64 Pet Treats
66 Rainbow Sugar Chart

# Educational Resources

## Educational Resources Index

**68** The Thrill of Skill
**69** Ten Tips for Baking Success
**70** Baking Skills Check List
**71** Measurement Guide
**71** Ingredient Substitution Guide
**72** Reading List for Baking Literature
**73** Baking Certificate
**74** Glossary

*Whether you are a teacher, mentor, or parent, these educational resources will enhance your experience of baking with children.*

# Designer Oatmeal Cookies

## Ingredients:

⅔ cup whole wheat or all-purpose flour
½ teaspoon baking powder
¼ teaspoon baking soda
½ teaspoon ground cinnamon
⅛ teaspoon salt
½ cup butter, softened
⅓ cup packed brown sugar
⅓ cup sugar
1 egg
½ teaspoon vanilla
1½ cups uncooked quick or old-fashioned oats
¾ cup chocolate baking chips or moist raisins or dried fruit*
½ cup chopped nuts or sunflower seeds, unsalted, roasted

*For moist dried raisins, soak raisins in water for 5 minutes and drain.

**Preparation Time:** 30 minutes
**Baking Time:** 8 to 10 minutes
**Makes:** 2 dozen
**Serving:** 1 cookie

# Directions:

1. Preheat oven to 375 °F.

2. Combine flour, baking powder, baking soda, cinnamon and salt in small mixing bowl.

3. Combine butter, brown sugar, sugar, egg and vanilla in large mixing bowl. Beat until creamy.

4. Add flour mixture and oats to creamed mixture and thoroughly combine.

5. Add baking chips or fruit and nuts.

6. Drop by teaspoonful onto an ungreased baking sheet. Bake 8 to 10 minutes. Cool on baking sheet for 2 minutes; remove to wire cooling rack to finish cooling.

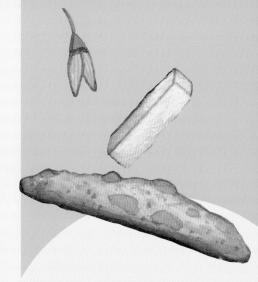

## Fun Fact:

Oats were once thought good only for horses and those with little money. It took a while for oats to be used in baking. One of the earliest oatmeal cookie recipes appeared in 1906.

## Family Activity:

This cookie combines the first (chocolate chip) and second (oatmeal raisin) most popular cookies in the U.S. Select optional ingredients to create your own family "designer" cookie. Package cookies to give as holiday gifts to relatives, neighbors, teachers, coaches and special friends.

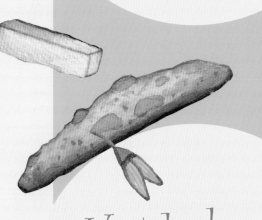

## Vocabulary

**Hospitable:** welcoming and generous to guests. Always try to be hospitable, the favor might be returned.

**Nutrition Facts (1 serving/29g)**
Calories: 118, Protein: 2g, Carbohydrates: 16g, Dietary Fiber: 1g, Fat: 6g, Saturated Fat: 3g, Mono Fat: 1g, Cholesterol: 19mg, Calcium: 12mg, Potassium: 63mg, Sodium: 65mg

# Forgotten Chocolate Chip Cookies

## Ingredients:

2 large egg whites, at room temperature
⅛ teaspoon salt
¾ teaspoon vanilla
⅔ cup sugar
⅔ cup mini semi-sweet chocolate chips

**Preparation Time:** 15 minutes
**Baking/finishing Time:** 5 to 6 hours or overnight
**Makes:** 3 dozen cookies
**Serving:** 1 cookie

# Directions:

**1.** Preheat oven to 350 °F.

**2.** Line two baking sheet pans with parchment paper or foil. (Do not spray or grease!)

**3.** Separate two large eggs, placing the whites in clean glass or stainless steel mixing bowl.

**4.** Beat the egg whites with salt and vanilla until foamy.

**5.** Gradually add the sugar while beating on high speed until the whites will hold a stiff peak.

**6.** Gently stir or fold in chocolate chips.

**7.** Using two teaspoons, lightly spoon 36 scoops of meringue onto the prepared baking sheet pans; space about an inch apart.

**8.** Place pans in preheated oven, shut the door and TURN OFF OVEN. Don't peek! Leave in the oven 5 to 6 hours or overnight.

**9.** Remove cooled pans from oven and cookies from the pans. Store in airtight container.

## Fun Fact:

In home baking, neither the shell color nor the grade of egg matter. The egg size for standard recipes is large unless stated otherwise.

## Family Activity:

Even small children can help spoon the meringue onto the baking sheet. Each child's name can be written in pencil on the parchment paper so they know where to place the meringue, and later find their cookie! Package these sweet puffs and deliver to a friend.

## Vocabulary:

**Kitchen:**
the place in a home where lives converge, are sustained and flourish.

**Nutrition Facts (1 serving/10g)**
Calories: 37, Carbohydrates: 6g, Fat: 1g, Saturated Fat: 1g, Calcium: 2mg, Potassium: 3mg, Sodium: 11mg

**Note: In each of the recipes in *Baking with Friends*, if the nutritional analysis was less than 0.5 the nutrient was not listed.**

# Fudge Brownies

## Ingredients:

½ cup butter or margarine (do not use a spread)
2 (1-ounce) squares unsweetened baking chocolate
1 cup sugar
¾ cup plus 2 tablespoons cake flour or ¾ cup all-purpose flour
2 eggs
½ cup chopped nuts

**Preparation Time:** 15 minutes
**Baking Time:** 20 to 25 minutes
**Makes:** 16 brownies
**Serving:** 1 brownie

# Directions:

**1.** Preheat oven to 350 °F.

**2.** Melt butter and unsweetened chocolate in 2-quart saucepan over medium-low heat, stirring constantly, until smooth.

**3.** Remove pan from heat and let cool 15 minutes.

**4.** Add sugar, flour, eggs and nuts to the chocolate mixture in the saucepan and mix until well blended.

**5.** Pour batter into greased or parchment-lined 9-inch square baking pan.

**6.** Bake 20 to 25 minutes or until brownie begins to pull away from the sides of the pan. (Do not over bake.)

**7.** Cool pan of brownies to room temperature on wire cooling rack before cutting.

## Fun Fact:

Chocolate was first manufactured in the United States in 1765, and was used as a health drink until around 1900. In 1906, the first brownie recipe was "Lowney's Brownies" in Boston.

## Family Activity:

Ask every family member, "What is your favorite cookie?" Find the recipe and take turns making everyone's favorite cookie. Freeze six cookies from every batch to create a cookie box to ship to military troops or give to a local emergency shelter.

## Vocabulary:

**Brownie:** a dense, chewy, cake-like cookie that is generally chocolate colored (hence the name); cut in bar shapes to serve.

**Nutrition Facts (1 serving/39g)**
Calories: 170, Protein: 2g, Carbohydrates: 19g, Dietary Fiber: 1g, Fat: 11g, Saturated Fat: 5g, Mono Fat: 2g, Poly Fat: 1g, Cholesterol: 42mg, Calcium: 10mg, Potassium: 58mg, Sodium: 57mg

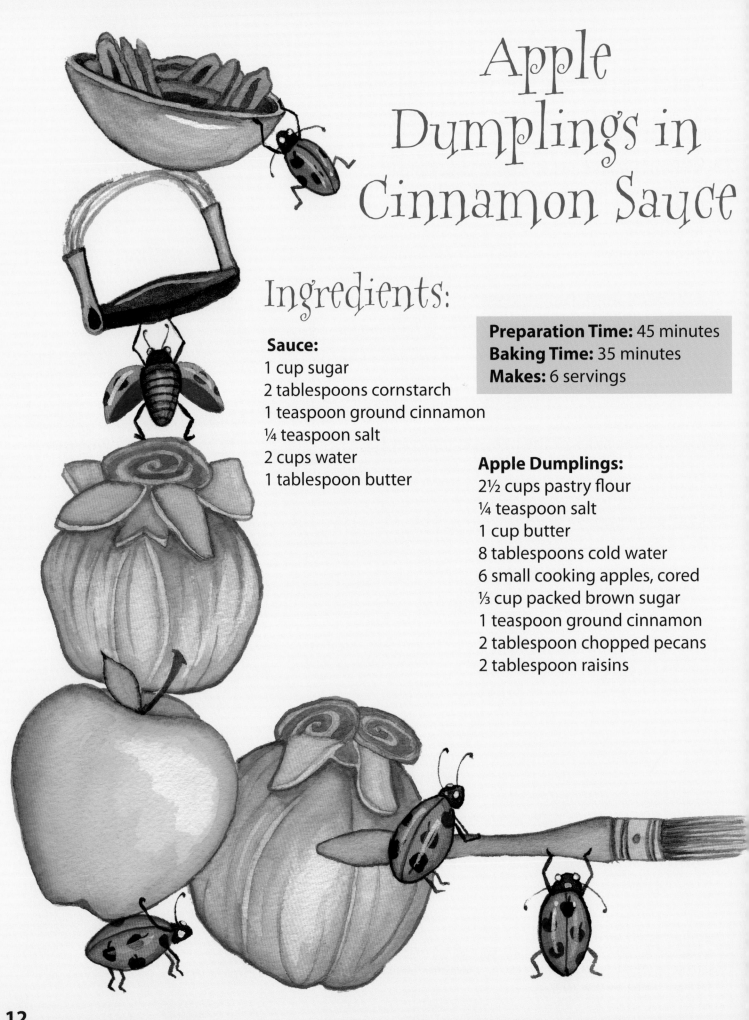

# Apple Dumplings in Cinnamon Sauce

## Ingredients:

**Preparation Time:** 45 minutes
**Baking Time:** 35 minutes
**Makes:** 6 servings

**Sauce:**
1 cup sugar
2 tablespoons cornstarch
1 teaspoon ground cinnamon
¼ teaspoon salt
2 cups water
1 tablespoon butter

**Apple Dumplings:**
2½ cups pastry flour
¼ teaspoon salt
1 cup butter
8 tablespoons cold water
6 small cooking apples, cored
⅓ cup packed brown sugar
1 teaspoon ground cinnamon
2 tablespoon chopped pecans
2 tablespoon raisins

# Directions:

1. Preheat oven to 375 °F.

2. To make sauce, combine sugar, cornstarch, cinnamon and salt in small saucepan.

3. Gradually stir in water and cook over medium heat until mixture begins to bubble and thicken about 5 minutes. Remove from heat and stir in 1 tablespoon butter; set aside.

4. To make the dumplings, combine pastry flour and salt in large mixing bowl.

5. Cut 1 cup butter into flour mixture using pastry blender, two knives or fork until mixture resembles coarse crumbs.

6. Stir in cold water, 1 tablespoon at a time, until mixture forms a ball.

7. Roll dough into 18x12-inch rectangle on lightly floured surface. Cut dough into six 6-inch squares. Place apple in center of each square.

8. Combine ⅓ cup brown sugar, 1 teaspoon cinnamon, pecans and raisins in small mixing bowl. Fill center of each apple with brown sugar mixture.

9. Pinch corners of dough together at top of apple; press edges together to seal.

10. Place apples in greased 13x9-inch baking dish.

11. Pour cinnamon sauce over apple dumplings. Bake for 35 to 45 minutes or until golden brown and apples are fork tender. Serve warm.

## Fun Fact:

Did you know there are more than 7,500 varieties of apples? More than 2,500 varieties are grown in the United States alone! That's a lot of apples!

# Family Activity:

Visit an apple orchard or farmer's market and find new varieties of apples for baking and eating. Purchase several varieties of apples and cut into slices for a family tasting! Which is your favorite?

## Vocabulary:

**Cut in:**
Blending together cold fat (shortening or butter) and flour or other ingredients by hand or with a pastry blender or a fork to create a mixture that appears crumbly or grainy.

**Nutrition Facts (1 serving/288g)**
Calories: 738, Protein: 5g, Carbohydrates: 106g, Dietary Fiber: 5g, Fat: 35g, Saturated Fat: 21g, Mono Fat: 9g, Poly Fat: 2g, Cholesterol: 86mg, Calcium: 37mg, Potassium: 255mg, Sodium 469mg

# Country Fruit Cobbler

## Ingredients:

4 cups sliced fresh or frozen peaches (about 8)
1 cup sugar, divided
¼ teaspoon ground cinnamon
½ cup all-purpose flour
½ cup white whole wheat flour
2 teaspoons baking powder
¼ teaspoon salt
1 cup milk
¼ cup melted butter

**Preparation Time:** 30 minutes
**Baking Time:** 50 to 60 minutes
**Makes:** 8 servings

# Directions:

**1.** Preheat oven to 350 °F.

**2.** Combine peaches, ½ cup sugar and cinnamon in large mixing bowl. Place peach mixture in greased 13x9-inch baking dish or iron skillet.

**3.** Combine ½ cup sugar, all-purpose flour, whole white wheat flour, baking powder and salt in medium mixing bowl.

**4.** Add milk and melted butter to dry mixture. Blend well.

**5.** Pour batter over peaches. Bake for 50 to 60 minutes or until crust is crisp and golden brown. Serve hot with ice cream or whipped cream.

## Fun Fact:

Cobblers are a simple traditional American dessert with many variations. The batter may be a biscuit, cake, dumpling or pie pastry placed on top or underneath the fruit. Fruits available vary, depending upon the season and local markets.

## Family Activity:

Cobbler recipes have been passed down through the generations. Visit with relatives and discover cobbler traditions in your family. You may find there are several versions! Visit a fruit farm and find fruits that are grown locally to make your cobbler.

## Vocabulary:

**Pandowdy**: deep dish apple dessert cooked with fruit under a biscuit dough crust.

**Nutrition Facts (1 serving/150g)**
Calories: 253, Protein: 4g, Carbohydrates: 46g, Dietary Fiber: 2g, Fat: 6g, Saturated Fat: 4g, Cholesterol: 17mg, Calcium: 69mg, Potassium: 156mg, Sodium: 275mg

# Gingerbread

## Ingredients:

2 cups whole wheat flour
½ cup all-purpose flour
¼ cup sugar
1 teaspoon baking soda
½ teaspoon salt
1½ teaspoons ground cinnamon
1½ teaspoons ground ginger
½ teaspoon ground cloves
1 cup buttermilk, plain yogurt or sour milk*
¾ cup molasses
⅓ cup melted butter or vegetable oil
2 tablespoons honey
2 eggs, beaten
Whipped cream, optional

*Option - Mix 2 tablespoons vinegar or lemon juice and additional milk to equal 1 cup.

**Preparation Time:** 15 minutes
**Baking Time:** 45 to 50 minutes
**Makes:** 9 squares
**Serving:** 1 square

# Directions:

**1.** Preheat oven to 350 °F.

**2.** Grease and lightly flour 8-inch square cake pan.

**3.** Combine whole wheat flour, all-purpose flour, sugar, baking soda, salt and spices in a medium mixing bowl.

**4.** Add buttermilk, molasses, butter, honey and beaten eggs to the dry mixture. Mix just until smooth.

**5.** Pour batter into the prepared cake pan. Bake 45 to 50 minutes or until wooden pick inserted in center comes out clean.

**6.** Cool 15 minutes or longer on wire cooling rack before serving. Serve warm with whipped cream.

## Fun Fact:

Early American colonists served Gingerbread because molasses came from trading with the West Indies. George Washington's mother served Gingerbread to Lafayette when he visited her in 1784!

## Family Activity:

How many times each week do you eat together as a family? Set a goal to turn off the TV and cell phones and eat together as a family five times weekly. Create a jar of "please tell me about…." questions for family conversation.

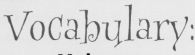

## Vocabulary:

**Molasses:** sweet syrupy by-product of processing sugar beets or sugar cane into sugar. The word molasses comes from a Portuguese word melaço, that comes from the Latin word for honey--"mel."

**Nutrition Facts (1 serving/119g)**
Calories: 321, Protein: 7g, Carbohydrates: 56g, Dietary Fiber: 4g, Fat: 9g, Saturated Fat: 5g, Mono Fat: 1g, Cholesterol: 68mg, Potassium: 575mg, Sodium: 378mg

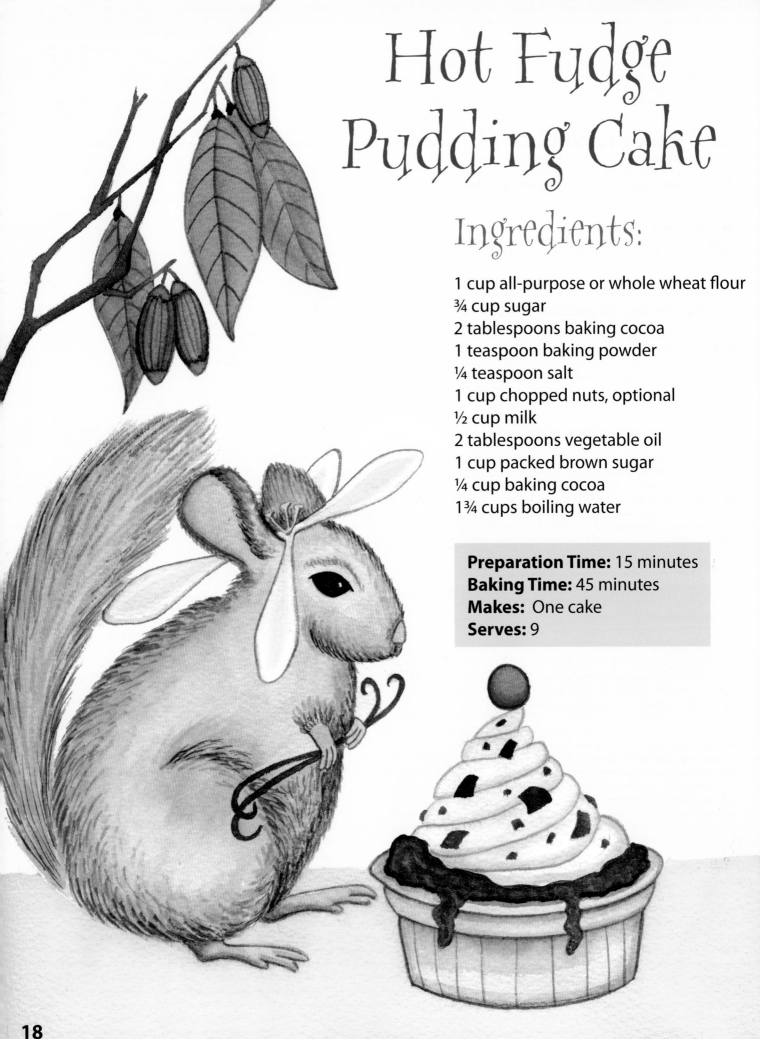

# Hot Fudge Pudding Cake

## Ingredients:

1 cup all-purpose or whole wheat flour
¾ cup sugar
2 tablespoons baking cocoa
1 teaspoon baking powder
¼ teaspoon salt
1 cup chopped nuts, optional
½ cup milk
2 tablespoons vegetable oil
1 cup packed brown sugar
¼ cup baking cocoa
1¾ cups boiling water

**Preparation Time:** 15 minutes
**Baking Time:** 45 minutes
**Makes:** One cake
**Serves:** 9

# Directions:

**1.** Preheat oven to 350 °F.

**2.** Grease 9-inch square baking pan.

**3.** Combine flour, sugar, 2 tablespoons baking cocoa, baking powder and salt in large mixing bowl.

**4.** Stir nuts, milk and vegetable oil into flour mixture. Spread batter into greased baking pan.

**5.** Combine brown sugar and ¼ cup baking cocoa in small mixing bowl. Sprinkle brown sugar and cocoa mixture over top of batter.

**6.** Place pan on middle oven rack.

**7.** Pour the boiling water over top of batter and brown sugar mixture. Bake 45 minutes. The cake rises and the chocolate sauce forms on the bottom! Serve warm with whipped cream or ice cream and berries.

## Family Activity:

Make this dessert together as a family before dinner. Bake it while you eat dinner and dessert will be ready warm from the oven for your family to enjoy!

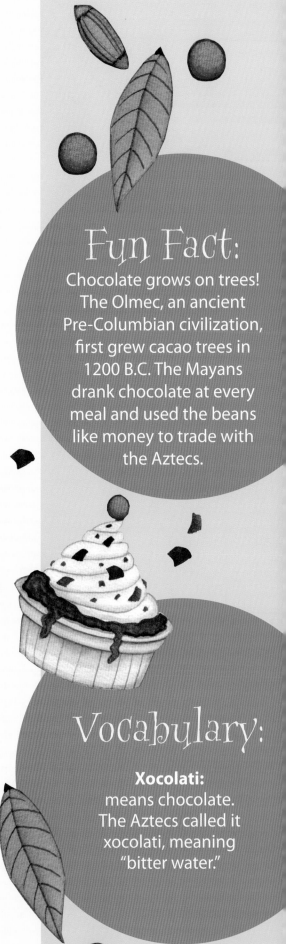

## Fun Fact:

Chocolate grows on trees! The Olmec, an ancient Pre-Columbian civilization, first grew cacao trees in 1200 B.C. The Mayans drank chocolate at every meal and used the beans like money to trade with the Aztecs.

## Vocabulary:

**Xocolati:**
means chocolate. The Aztecs called it xocolati, meaning "bitter water."

**Nutrition Facts (1 serving/84g) with nuts**
Calories: 316, Protein: 4g, Carbohydrates: 52g, Dietary Fiber: 3g, Fat: 12g,
Saturated Fat: 1g, Mono Fat: 7g, Poly Fat: 4g, Calcium: 41mg,
Potassium: 184mg, Sodium: 133mg,

# Lazy Daisy Cake

## Ingredients:

**Cake Ingredients:**
2 cups sugar
4 eggs
2 teaspoons vanilla
½ teaspoon salt
2 tablespoons butter or margarine, softened
1 cup steaming hot milk (190 °F)
2 cups all-purpose flour
2 teaspoons baking powder

**Broiled Icing Ingredients:**
6 tablespoons butter or margarine
4 tablespoons cream or evaporated milk
¾ cup packed brown sugar
1 cup chopped pecans, coconut or corn flakes

**Preparation Time:** 20 minutes
**Baking Time:** 30 to 35 minutes
**Makes:** One cake
**Serves:** 24

# Directions:

1. Preheat oven to 350 °F.

2. Grease and flour the bottom of 13x9-inch cake pan.

3. Combine sugar, eggs, vanilla and salt in large mixing bowl. Beat until lemon colored and sugar is dissolved, about 5 minutes. Do not under beat.

4. While beating eggs, heat milk to steaming hot. Remove from heat. Melt butter in steaming hot milk.

5. Combine flour and baking powder in medium mixing bowl. Add the flour mixture into the egg mixture and mix well.

6. Add hot milk and butter mixture to batter and mix just until combined.

7. Immediately pour batter into prepared pan. Bake 30 to 35 minutes or until wooden pick inserted in center comes out clean.

8. While cake bakes, prepare icing. Combine all icing ingredients in small mixing bowl. Mixture will not be smooth.

9. Spread icing over warm cake. Turn broiler unit on in oven and place cake on rack 3 inches from heat. Broil for 3 minutes with oven door slightly open while you watch. Remove cake from oven as soon as mixture bubbles and browns. Watch carefully as it can burn easily!

## Fun Fact:

Home bakers all over the United States were baking the Lazy Daisy Cake in the 1960's. Why is it called Lazy Daisy Cake? Create a story to go with this legendary cake!

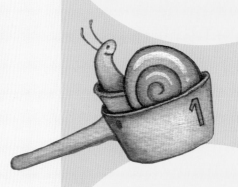

## Family Activity:

Interview relatives to discover foods or recipes that may be a tradition in your family or local community that you could learn to bake or cook! Learn everything about the recipe so it is not "lost!"

## Vocabulary:

**Legend:**
a story handed down from the past, often passed from generation to generation.

**Nutrition Facts (1 serving/65g)**
Calories: 212, Protein: 3g, Carbohydrates: 32g, Dietary Fiber: 1g, Fat: 8g, Saturated Fat: 3g, Mono Fat: 3g, Poly Fat: 1g, Cholesterol: 47mg, Calcium: 37mg, Potassium: 50mg, Sodium: 141mg,

# Old-Fashioned Apple Cake Dessert

## Ingredients:

2 cups sugar
½ cup butter, softened
2 eggs
1 teaspoon vanilla
2 cups all-purpose flour
2 teaspoons baking soda
1 teaspoon ground cinnamon
½ teaspoon ground nutmeg
¼ teaspoon salt
¼ cup milk
4 cups chopped unpeeled apples (about 4 medium apples)
½ cup raisins
½ cup chopped pecans

**Preparation Time:** 30 minutes
**Baking Time:** 50 to 60 minutes
**Makes:** One cake
**Serves:** 12

**Optional Vanilla Sauce for topping:**
> 1 cup sugar
> 3 tablespoons all-purpose flour
> 1 cup water
> ½ cup butter
> 1 teaspoon vanilla

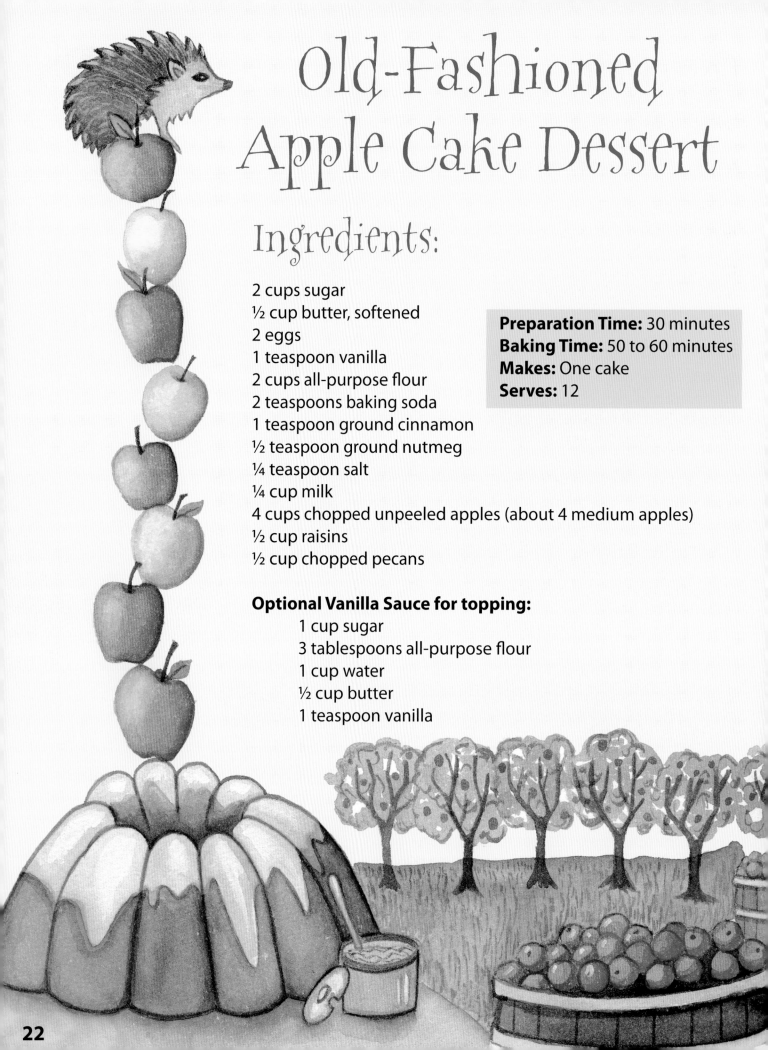

# Directions:

**1.** Preheat oven to 325 °F.

**2.** Grease bottom and sides of 13x9-inch pan.

**3.** Combine sugar and butter in large mixing bowl until light and fluffy. Add eggs and vanilla; blend well.

**4.** Combine flour, baking soda, cinnamon, nutmeg and salt in a separate bowl and add to creamed mixture with ¼ cup milk.

**5.** Stir in apples, raisins and pecans; mix well. Pour batter into greased pan.

**6.** Bake 50 to 60 minutes or until wooden pick inserted in center comes out clean.

**Optional Vanilla Sauce:** Thoroughly blend sugar and flour in medium saucepan. Slowly add water while stirring mixture. Add butter and cook over medium heat until mixture begins to boil. Continue boiling five minutes, stirring constantly; add vanilla. Remove from heat and let stand about 5 minutes before drizzling sauce over warm cake.

## Fun Fact:

Early settlers treasured apple seeds. Whenever people settled, they planted an apple tree in their yard to have fruit.

# Family Activity:

Etiquette Tip - When dessert is served, everyone should wait to eat their dessert until the host/hostess is re-seated and takes their first bite. Then everyone may enjoy!

## Vocabulary:

**"Wind falls:"** apples that fell off the trees. These apples were washed, cleaned and crushed for cider or prepared in pie, crisp, cake, apple butter, jelly, or made into applesauce.

**Nutrition Facts (1 serving/132g) without sauce**
Calories: 363, Protein: 4g, Carbohydrates: 62g, Dietary Fiber: 2g,
Fat: 12g, Saturated Fat: 5g, Mono Fat: 4g, Poly Fat: 1g, Cholesterol: 57mg,
Calcium: 21mg, Potassium: 150mg, Sodium: 329mg

# Quilt Patch Cake

## Ingredients:

**Yellow Cake**
1½ cups sugar
½ cup butter, softened
3 eggs
1 teaspoon vanilla
2¼ cups cake flour
3 teaspoons baking powder
½ teaspoon salt
1 cup milk

## Directions:

**1.** Preheat oven to 350 °F.

**2.** Combine sugar and butter in large mixing bowl and beat until light and creamy.

**3.** Add eggs, one at a time, mixing well after each addition.

**4.** Stir in vanilla.

**5.** Combine cake flour, baking powder and salt in separate mixing bowl.

**6.** Gradually add combined dry ingredients alternately with milk to creamed sugar mixture.

**7.** Pour batter into greased and floured 13x9-inch baking pan. Bake for 30 to 35 minutes or until wooden pick inserted in center comes out clean.

**8.** Cool completely before decorating.

**Preparation Time:** 30 minutes
**Baking Time:** 30 to 35 minutes
**Makes:** One cake
**Serves:** 12

# Quilt Patch Cake Decorations

**Ingredients:**
3 cups powdered sugar
⅓ cup butter or margarine, softened
1½ teaspoons vanilla
2 to 3 tablespoons milk
Piped frosting, string candy or fruit leather
Colored frosting
Colored sugar (See Rainbow Sugar Chart page 66)
Candies, nuts or dried fruits

**Directions to Decorate Cake:**

**1.** Combine powdered sugar and butter in medium mixing bowl and mix until light and fluffy.

**2.** Stir in vanilla and gradually add milk. Beat until smooth and spreading consistency. Divide and color for decorating, as desired.

**3.** Frost the surface of the cooled cake with a thin layer of white frosting.

**4.** Divide the cake with piped frosting or string candy or fruit leather into 12 even squares to create a patch quilt pattern on the top of the cake.

**5.** Decorate each square with frosting, colored sugar, candies, nuts, dried fruits to create quilt patterns on the cake.

## Fun Fact:

American folk art includes many shapes and colors to create quilt patterns. Quilts were a way to make "something out of nothing" using leftover scraps of fabric to create a beautiful pattern.

# Family Activity:

Let each family member decorate a square for a family quilt cake. Use triangles and other patterns cut from baking parchment paper as stencils to help make designs.

## Vocabulary:

**Quilt:**
a bed cover filled with down or cotton and stitched together in lines and patterns that often have a theme or tell a story.

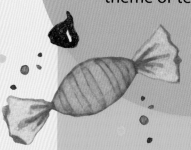

**Nutrition Facts (1 serving/131g) cake with frosting**
Calories: 434, Protein: 4g, Carbohydrates: 73g, Fat: 14g, Saturated Fat: 9g,
Mono Fat: 4g, Poly Fat: 1g, Cholesterol: 89mg, Calcium: 67mg,
Potassium: 42mg, Sodium: 357mg;

# Rustic Country Fruit Tart

## Ingredients:

1½ cups pastry or all-purpose flour*
¼ teaspoon salt
½ cup cold butter
1 teaspoon cider vinegar, optional
4 to 5 tablespoons cold water
½ cup packed brown sugar
¼ cup cornstarch
1 teaspoon ground cinnamon
Pinch ground nutmeg
2½ cups peeled and sliced tart pie apples
1½ cups fresh, frozen or dried tart cherries
2 tablespoon cold butter, cut into small pieces

*Pastry flour may be whole wheat or enriched flour.

**Preparation Time:** Crust 10 minutes, fruit 15 minutes
**Baking Time:** 40 to 50 minutes
**Makes:** One tart
**Serves:** 8

## Directions:

**1.** Preheat oven to 375 °F.

**2.** Combine flour and salt in medium bowl.

**3.** Cut ½ cup butter into flour mixture using pastry blender, fork or two knives until mixture resembles coarse crumbs.

**4.** Stir vinegar into ice water and sprinkle 3 to 5 tablespoons of cold water over flour mixture, tossing with a fork, until the mixture is moistened.

**5.** Press the dough together into a disc, about 1½ - inch thick and four inches across. Wrap the disc in plastic wrap, waxed paper or parchment and refrigerate up to 4 hours or overnight OR freeze to firm.

**6.** Combine brown sugar, cornstarch, cinnamon and nutmeg in large mixing bowl. Add fruit and stir to coat with sugar mixture.

**7.** Roll crust pastry into 12- to 14-inch circle and place on ungreased baking sheet pan, pie pan or oven safe plate.

**8.** Place fruit filling in center of crust, heaping it up in the middle; dot with 2 tablespoons butter and pull crust up 2 to 3 inches over the filling, all around the circle, overlapping dough slightly.

**9.** Press overlapping dough gently, leaving a 4-5-inch center circle open with fruit showing. Brush crust with milk; sprinkle with sugar.

**10.** Bake at 40 to 50 minutes. Cool on wire rack 15 to 20 minutes or more.

## Family Activity:

To make hand held pies: On Step 5 make four small discs. Roll out each small disc to 6-inches across; place 2 inches apart on baking sheet lined with parchment paper. Fill with fruit and dot with 1 teaspoon butter for each tart. Pull up dough leaving a small 1-inch opening. Sprinkle with sugar and bake 20 to 25 minutes.

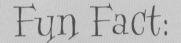

## Fun Fact:

The most favored pie in the United States of America is Apple Pie!

## Vocabulary:

**Fruit Tart:**
an open crust pastry, topped with sweetened fruit.

**Nutrition Facts (1 serving/109g)**
Calories: 348, Protein: 3g, Carbohydrates: 52g, Dietary Fiber: 9g, Fat: 15g, Saturated Fat: 9g, Mono Fat: 4g, Cholesterol: 38mg, Calcium: 32mg, Potassium: 93mg; Sodium: 177mg

# Confetti Cornbread

## Ingredients:

1 cup white, yellow or whole grain cornmeal
1 cup all-purpose flour
1 or 2 tablespoons sugar, optional
2½ teaspoons baking powder
½ teaspoon salt
1 egg
1 cup low-fat milk or skim milk
3 tablespoons melted butter or vegetable oil
1 cup shredded Cheddar cheese or reduced fat cheese
⅓ cup chopped green onions
⅓ cup chopped green, red or yellow peppers

**Preparation Time:** 10 minutes
**Baking Time:** 25 to 30 minutes
**Makes:** 12 squares or wedges

# Directions:

1. Preheat oven to 425 °F.

2. Grease bottom and sides of 9-inch square or round baking pan.

3. Combine cornmeal, flour, sugar, baking powder and salt in medium mixing bowl.

4. Beat egg with fork or whisk in separate small mixing bowl. Add milk and melted butter, beating well.

5. Add egg mixture to dry ingredients; mix only until dry ingredients are combined.

6. Stir in cheese, onions and peppers. Do not over mix, the batter will not be smooth. Pour batter into greased pan.

7. Bake 25 to 30 minutes until golden brown and wooden pick inserted in center comes out clean.

**Option:** Pour batter into greased muffin cups. Bake 18 to 20 minutes. Makes 12 muffins.

## Fun Fact:

Corn is a grain and staple crop of ancient cultures in the Americas cultivated as early as 300 B.C.

# Family Activity:

Beginning bakers can use a cornbread baking mix and learn measuring, mixing and portioning skills.

## Vocabulary:

**Cornmeal:** dried yellow, blue or white corn kernels ground into fine, medium or coarse meal. Cornmeal may be degerminated or wholegrain.

**Nutrition Facts (1 serving/66g)**
Calories: 154, Protein: 6g, Carbohydrates: 18g, Dietary Fiber: 1g, Fat: 7g, Saturated Fat: 3g, Mono Fat: 1g, Cholesterol: 36mg, Calcium: 120mg, Potassium: 101mg, Sodium: 313mg

# Crispy Whole Grain
# Waffles

## Ingredients:

1⅔ cups whole wheat flour
⅓ cup cornmeal or favorite multigrain hot cereal
¼ cup cornstarch
1 tablespoon sugar
4 teaspoons baking powder
1 teaspoon baking soda
¼ teaspoon salt
3 eggs, beaten
2 cups buttermilk*
½ cup melted butter or vegetable oil

*Option - Mix 2 tablespoons vinegar or lemon juice and additional milk to equal 2 cups.

**Preparation Time:** 20 minutes
**Baking Time:** Check manufacturer's recommendation
**Makes:** 16 waffles
**Serving:** 1 waffle

# Directions:

**1.** Brush waffle iron with oil and preheat as directed by manufacturer.

**2.** Combine flour, cornmeal, cornstarch, sugar, baking powder, baking soda and salt in large mixing bowl.

**3.** Combine eggs, buttermilk and melted butter in separate mixing bowl.

**4.** Add liquid mixture to dry mixture. Stir just to blend.

**5.** Bake in waffle iron until crispy brown or as waffle iron instructions direct.

## Fun Fact:

Before Meriweather Lewis left on the Lewis and Clark expedition, he visited Thomas Jefferson in Washington D.C. (1801-1803). Jefferson introduced Lewis to a new food – waffles.

## Family Activity:

Make a special day even better! Let the birthday honoree plan their breakfast menu. Prepare the breakfast as a family and serve the birthday breakfast in bed to the family member as a treat to honor their birthday!

## Vocabulary:

**Cornstarch:**
the dense fine white flour obtained from the center (endosperm) of corn kernels. When mixed with wheat flour in cakes, cookies and waffles, it produces a finer textured product.

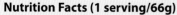

**Nutrition Facts (1 serving/66g)**
Calories: 155, Protein: 4g, Carbohydrates: 16g, Dietary Fiber: 2g, Fat: 9g, Saturated Fat: 1g, Mono Fat: 4g, Poly Fat: 3g, Cholesterol: 43mg, Calcium: 77mg, Potassium: 124mg, Sodium: 293mg

# Flour Tortillas

## Ingredients:

2½ cups unbleached all-purpose flour
  (may use half whole wheat flour)
1 teaspoon salt
1 teaspoon baking powder
1 to 1¼ cups warm water (105 °F)
2 tablespoons vegetable oil

**Preparation Time:** 30 minutes
**Baking Time:** 1½ to 2 minutes
**Makes:** 8 tortillas
**Serving:** 1 tortilla

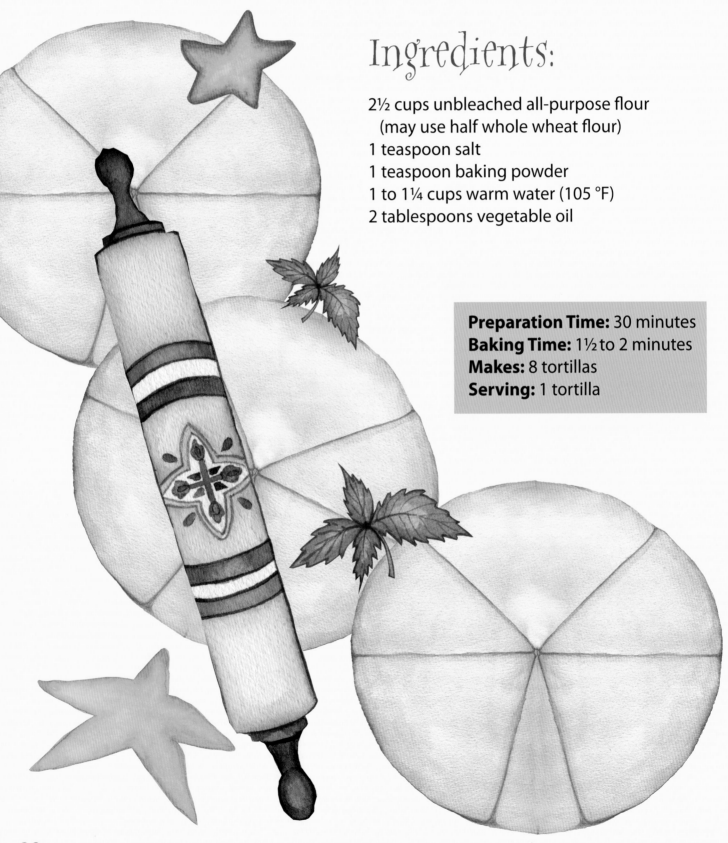

# Directions:

**1.** Combine flour, salt and baking powder in large mixing bowl.

**2.** Add warm water and oil to flour mixture. Stir until mixture is blended and sticks together. If dough is too sticky, add small sprinkles of flour. Knead dough lightly to form a smooth dough ball. If dough is dry, add small sprinkles of water.

**3.** Divide dough into eight pieces; shape each dough piece into a ball. Let rest covered or in plastic bag for 15 to 20 minutes or refrigerate overnight.

**4.** Flatten each ball into a thin circle about 8 to 10 inches across using a rolling pin or hands.

**5.** Heat griddle or skillet to medium hot. Bake each tortilla about 1½ to 2 minutes per side or until lightly browned.

**Baker's Tip:** Tortilla will have brown speckled spots. Stack, cover and keep warm.

## Fun Fact:
Tortillas are the cornerstone of the Mexican diet—morning, noon and night. In Mexico, corn tortillas are most commonly eaten. In the U.S., the flour tortilla is the most popular variety.

## Family Activity:

What is your favorite bread? Let every family member name their favorite. (Answers may include pancakes, tortillas, crackers, raisin bread, sliced bread or buns, muffins, bagels, pita, flat bread…)

## Vocabulary:

**Baker's Dozen:** thirteen items. In feudal times, bakers provided an extra item so the hungry servant who received the court's bread would not be tempted to steal; making the order "short."

**Nutrition Facts (1 serving/44g)**
Calories: 174, Protein: 4g, Carbohydrates: 30g, Dietary Fiber: 1g, Fat: 3g, Saturated Fat: 1g, Mono Fat: 2g, Poly Fat: 2g, Calcium: 18mg, Potassium: 41mg, Sodium: 365mg

# Katy's A+ Crepes

## Ingredients:

¾ cup pastry or white whole wheat flour
¼ cup all-purpose flour
1 tablespoon sugar
⅛ teaspoon salt
1 cup 1% milk
4 large eggs
1 teaspoon vegetable oil
2 cups vanilla low-fat yogurt or favorite flavor
1½ cups sliced fruit or berries
Powdered sugar for sprinkling

**Preparation Time:** 10 minutes
**Batter Rest Time:** 30 minutes to overnight
**Cook Time:** 15 minutes
**Makes:** 12 medium crepes
**Serving:** 1 crepe

# Directions:

**1.** Combine pastry and all purpose flour, sugar and salt in medium mixing bowl.

**2.** Combine milk and eggs until smooth in a separate medium mixing bowl.

**3.** Add egg mixture to flour mixture and whisk until smooth.

**4.** Set aside for 30 minutes or refrigerate batter overnight.

**5.** Grease non-stick 8 or 10-inch skillet or crepe pan with vegetable oil. Heat until the surface will sizzle with a drop of water.

**6.** Pour or ladle 2 tablespoons of batter into hot pan. Turn the pan until the bottom is evenly coated with batter. Place the pan back on the burner and cook just until the batter is set and lightly browned on the underside. Flip the crepe using a spatula until the other side is lightly browned. Transfer crepe to platter and repeat with remaining batter.

**7.** Spoon ⅛ cup yogurt and two tablespoons of fruit down the center of each crepe; roll up. Sprinkle with powdered sugar, if desired.

## Fun Fact:
Many varieties occur in crepes. Savory crepes are filled with meat, cheeses or vegetable mixtures. Dessert crepes may be spread with a jam or fruit mixture, rolled or folded!

## Vocabulary:
**Crepe:**
French word for a thin pancake rolled and filled. This dish is a staple of French cuisine.

# Family Activity:

Make a fruit topping for yogurt, waffles or pancakes. Melt 2 tablespoons orange marmalade and blend with 2 cups sliced strawberries, blueberries or raspberries.

**Nutrition Facts (1 serving/105g) with filling**
Calories: 127, Protein: 5g, Carbohydrates: 19g, Dietary Fiber: 2g, Fat: 3g, Saturated Fat: 1g, Mono Fat: 1g, Cholesterol: 76mg, Calcium: 109mg, Sodium: 80mg

# Pumpkin Pancakes

## Ingredients:

1 cup all-purpose or wholegrain baking mix
¼ cup quick oatmeal or whole wheat flour or
    cornmeal or flax meal
1 tablespoon packed dark brown sugar
¼ teaspoon ground cinnamon
⅛ teaspoon ground nutmeg
⅛ teaspoon ground ginger
¾ cup low fat milk
¼ cup cooked or canned pumpkin
1 egg, lightly beaten
1 tablespoon melted butter
Vegetable oil

**Preparation Time:** 10 minutes
**Baking Time:** 2-3 minutes per side
**Makes:** 15 pancakes
**Serving:** 1 pancake

# Directions:

**1.** Preheat griddle or skillet until hot (400 °F).

**2.** Combine baking mix, oatmeal, brown sugar and spices in medium mixing bowl.

**3.** Combine milk, pumpkin, egg and butter in separate bowl. Add to dry ingredients and mix just until blended. Do not over mix.

**4.** Brush griddle or skillet with vegetable oil. Griddle or skillet is ready for pancakes when a drop of water sprinkled on the hot surface sizzles.

**5.** Ladle or pour ¼ cup batter for each pancake onto the griddle or skillet. Space batter 2 inches apart for easier flipping.

**6.** Bake until tops are bubbly and edges are dry. Turn pancakes only once; bake until golden brown. Serve with fruit sauce, applesauce, honey, pumpkin butter or syrup.

# Family Activity:

Make a Pumpkin Butter to spread on the pancakes. In a large saucepan, combine one (29 ounce) can pumpkin, ¾ cup apple juice, 1½ cups sugar, 2 teaspoons ground cinnamon, ¾ teaspoon EACH ground ginger and ground nutmeg and ½ teaspoon ground cloves. Slowly bring to boil and simmer while stirring, about 30 minutes until thick. Serve warm or refrigerate when cooled.

# Fun Fact:
The first recipe for a pancake appeared in an English cookbook back in the fifteenth century.

# Vocabulary:

**Self-rising flour:** a blend of all-purpose flour, baking powder and salt.

**Nutrition Facts (1 serving/31g)**
Calories: 58, Protein: 2g, Carbohydrates: 9g, Dietary Fiber: 1g, Fat: 2g, Mono Fat: 1g, Cholesterol: 15mg, Calcium: 19mg, Potassium: 18mg, Sodium: 11mg

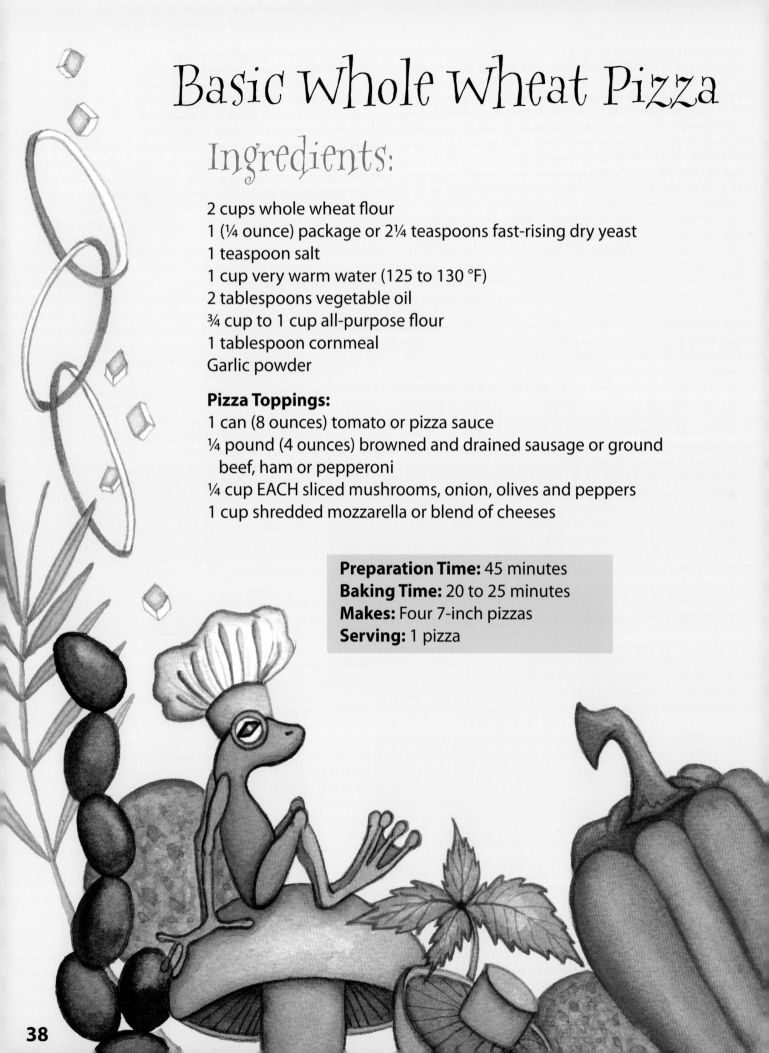

# Basic Whole Wheat Pizza

## Ingredients:

2 cups whole wheat flour
1 (¼ ounce) package or 2¼ teaspoons fast-rising dry yeast
1 teaspoon salt
1 cup very warm water (125 to 130 °F)
2 tablespoons vegetable oil
¾ cup to 1 cup all-purpose flour
1 tablespoon cornmeal
Garlic powder

**Pizza Toppings:**
1 can (8 ounces) tomato or pizza sauce
¼ pound (4 ounces) browned and drained sausage or ground
  beef, ham or pepperoni
¼ cup EACH sliced mushrooms, onion, olives and peppers
1 cup shredded mozzarella or blend of cheeses

**Preparation Time:** 45 minutes
**Baking Time:** 20 to 25 minutes
**Makes:** Four 7-inch pizzas
**Serving:** 1 pizza

# Directions:

**1.** Preheat oven to 450 °F.

**2.** Combine 2 cups whole wheat flour, yeast and salt in large mixing bowl.

**3.** Add water and vegetable oil to flour mixture. Stir until ingredients are blended.

**4.** Stir in enough remaining all-purpose flour until dough forms a ball and pulls away from sides of the bowl.

**5.** Knead dough in bowl or on lightly floured surface about 4 to 6 minutes or until dough is smooth and elastic.

**6.** Divide into four even pieces, shape into smooth balls. Place bowl over dough pieces and allow to rest 10 minutes.

**7.** Prepare toppings.

**8.** Lightly oil baking sheets. Sprinkle with cornmeal. Use hands to pat dough pieces into flat round crusts on baking sheets so they are not touching. Allow dough to rest if needed. Pinch to form an edge.

**9.** Sprinkle crust with garlic powder.

**10.** Select toppings. For one personal pan pizza spread ¼ can sauce over crust. Top with one-fourth of meat, and one tablespoon of EACH vegetable topping and ¼ cup shredded cheese.

**11.** Bake for 20 to 25 minutes or until crust is golden brown.

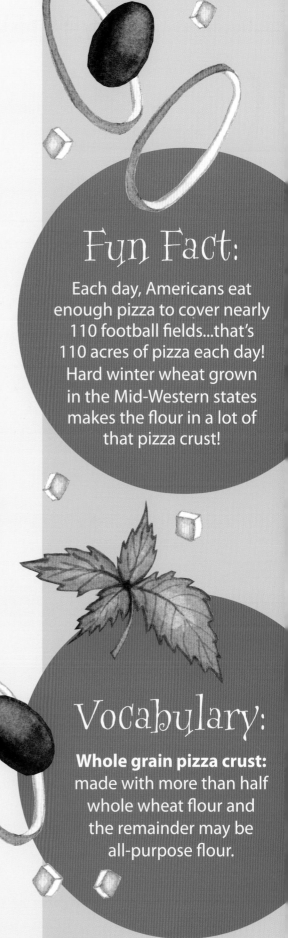

## Fun Fact:

Each day, Americans eat enough pizza to cover nearly 110 football fields...that's 110 acres of pizza each day! Hard winter wheat grown in the Mid-Western states makes the flour in a lot of that pizza crust!

## Vocabulary:

**Whole grain pizza crust:** made with more than half whole wheat flour and the remainder may be all-purpose flour.

## Family Activity:

Start a family tradition by making homemade pizza one night a week. Each family member can make their own unique pizza.

**Nutrition Facts (1 serving/155g) without topping**
Calories: 363, Protein: 12g, Carbohydrates: 64g, Dietary Fiber: 9g, Fat: 9g, Saturated Fat: 1g, Mono Fat: 3g, Poly Fat: 4g, Calcium: 26mg, Potassium: 319mg, Sodium: 595mg

# Chicken and Dumpling Soup

*Surprise! Not all quick breads are baked... these dumplings are steamed in the chicken stock!*

## Soup Ingredients:

4 large chicken breasts (about 2 pounds),
  cut into 1-inch pieces
4 cups chicken broth
4 cups water
4 medium potatoes, peeled and quartered
1 onion, chopped
4 carrots, peeled and quartered
½ teaspoon salt
¼ teaspoon black pepper

## Dumpling Ingredients:

1 cup all–purpose flour
¼ cup yellow cornmeal
2 teaspoons baking powder
¼ teaspoon salt
1 egg
¾ cup milk
2 tablespoons butter, melted

**Preparation Time:** 1½ hours
**Baking Time:** 30 to 35 minutes
**Makes:** 8 servings

# Directions:

**1.** Place chicken, broth, water, potatoes, onions, carrots, salt and pepper in Dutch oven or large saucepan. Cover and cook 45 minutes or until chicken and vegetables are tender.

**2.** To make dumplings combine flour, cornmeal, baking powder and salt in medium bowl.

**3.** Beat egg and milk in small mixing bowl. Add egg mixture and melted butter to flour mixture; mix only until flour mixture is combined.

**4.** Gently place tablespoons of dough on top of the boiling soup. Makes 8 dumplings or 16 smaller dumplings.

**5.** Cover pan tightly. Do not peek during cooking time. (Steam and heat will escape.)

**6.** Return pan to high heat and bring to a boil; reduce heat to medium and cook 10 to 15 minutes.

## Fun Fact:
A dumpling is found in many ethnic groups. One of the simplest is the Jewish Matzoh balls dropped into broth. Many Asian cultures have steamed dumplings; dough filled with chopped vegetables meat or fish, then steamed.

## Family Activity:

Enjoy reading all about dumplings from other cultures. Check the library for *Dumpling Soup* by Jama Kim Rattigan, then create your own family Dumpling Holiday to celebrate each year.

## Vocabulary:

**Dumpling:**
small amount of dough, usually shaped into a ball and cooked by boiling or steaming.

**Nutrition Facts (1 serving/410g)**
Calories: 325, Protein: 32g, Carbohydrates: 35g, Dietary Fiber: 3g, Fat: 6g, Saturated Fat: 3g, Mono Fat: 1g, Poly Fat: 1g, Cholesterol: 102mg, Calcium: 95mg, Potassium: 812mg, Sodium 965mg

# Cheese Quesadillas

## Ingredients:

1 cup (8 ounces) shredded Colby Jack or blend of cheeses
½ cup chopped tomatoes
¼ cup chopped onions
¼ cup chopped bell peppers
1 can (14 ounces) black beans, rinsed and drained
1 tablespoon chopped fresh cilantro
8 (10-inch) soft flour tortillas (see Flour Tortillas page 32)

**Preparation Time:** 20 minutes
**Baking Time:** 5 minutes
**Makes:** 4 quesadillas
**Serving:** 1 quesadilla

# Directions:

**1.** Combine cheese, tomatoes, onions and peppers in medium bowl for filling.

**2.** Add black beans and cilantro to filling mixture, if desired.

**3.** Spray or oil skillet or griddle; heat until medium hot about 325 °F.

**4.** Place tortilla on the hot griddle. Spread ¼ of the filling ingredients on the tortilla and place another tortilla on top.

**5.** Bake each quesadilla 2 to 3 minutes per side until brown on each side.

**6.** Cool slightly, cut into wedges and serve. Serve with salsa, chopped olives or sour cream, if desired.

## Fun Fact:

As people try other culture's foods, these food names will often become part of everyday language. Quesadilla and tortilla are good examples.

## Family Activity:

Can you name the cultures, country and/or language from which your family's favorite foods originate? American cuisine is a surprising mixture of many international dishes.

## Vocabulary:

**Queso:**
(pronounced KAY-soh) means cheese in Spanish.

**Nutrition Facts (1 serving/294g)**
Calories: 602, Protein: 24g, Carbohydrates: 78g, Dietary Fiber: 8g,
Fat: 23g, Saturated Fat: 10g, Mono Fat: 3g, Poly Fat: 3g, Cholesterol: 47mg,
Calcium: 452mg, Potassium: 469mg; Sodium: 1,294mg

# 100% Whole Wheat Bread

## Ingredients:

2 cups water (80 °F)
1 (¼ ounce) package or 2¼ teaspoons active dry yeast
2 tablespoons honey, molasses or sugar
6 cups whole wheat flour
2 eggs
¼ cup melted butter or vegetable oil
2 teaspoons salt

**Preparation Time:** 2 hours
**Baking Time:** 30 to 35 minutes
**Makes:** 2 loaves; 16 slices per loaf
**Serving:** 1 slice

## Directions:

**1.** Combine water, yeast, honey and 3 cups whole wheat flour in large mixing bowl. Mix well for about 3 minutes. Cover; let stand 15 minutes or up to overnight (in the refrigerator).

**2.** Stir or mix down the yeast mixture (sponge dough). Add eggs, melted butter and salt. Mix until well blended.

**3.** Stir in enough remaining flour until dough forms a rough ball and pulls away from sides of the bowl.

**4.** Place dough on lightly floured surface; knead about 10 minutes until smooth and elastic. Place dough into large greased bowl; turn dough, greased-side is up.

**5.** Cover; let rise about 30 minutes or until double in size in a warm place (80 °F).

**6.** Divide dough in half and shape into two loaves. Place in two greased 8½ x 4 ½-inch pans, cover with damp clean non-terry towel and let dough expand to just above the tops of the pan.

**7.** Preheat oven to 350 °F. Bake 30 to 35 minutes or until center of loaf is 200-210 °F when tested with a thermometer.

**8.** Cool loaves on wire cooling racks about 30 minutes before wrapping or slicing.

**Options:** Scald 1½ cups milk, cool and substitute for 1½ cups of water.

## Fun Fact:

The many varieties of wheat are grouped in six classes (hard red or white winter, hard red or white spring, soft white, durum and soft red winter). The hard wheats, white or red, are best for making loaves of bread for slicing.

## Family Activity:

Make raisin bread by kneading 2 cups raisins or dried cherries or cranberries into dough or try adding 2 cups chopped and toasted walnuts as you shape loaves.

## Vocabulary:

**Kneading:**
Working with dough with the heels of your hands by pressing and folding it and turning the dough a quarter turn after each press and fold. Add as little flour as possible while kneading.

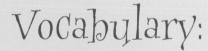

**Nutrition Facts (1 serving/29g)**
Calories: 98, Protein: 4g, Carbohydrates: 17g, Dietary Fiber: 3g, Fat: 2g, Cholesterol: 17mg, Calcium: 9mg, Potassium: 101mg, Sodium: 165mg

# Bread Sticks

## Ingredients:

1½ cups warm water (95 °F)
1 (¼ ounce) package or 2¼ teaspoons active dry yeast
½ cup cornmeal
4 to 4½ cups all-purpose flour (May be part whole wheat)
2 tablespoons vegetable oil
1½ teaspoons salt

**Optional:** Egg wash and cheese, sesame seeds or coarse salt.

**Preparation Time:** 40 to 50 minutes
**Baking Time:** 3 to 8 minutes
**Makes:** 16 bread sticks
**Serving:** 1 bread stick

# Directions:

**1.** Combine water, yeast, cornmeal and 2 cups of flour in large mixing bowl. Stir about 2 minutes. Cover; let stand 15 to 30 minutes.

**2.** Add vegetable oil, salt and 1 cup additional flour. Mix until well blended.

**3.** Add enough of the remaining flour until dough forms a rough ball and pulls away from sides of the bowl.

**4.** Place dough on lightly floured surface; knead about 5 minutes until smooth and elastic. Shape into a smooth round ball; cover; let dough rest 20 minutes OR place in greased bowl, cover and refrigerate until ready for shaping, up to 2 days. (Punch dough and reshape into dough ball each time it doubles.)

**5.** Divide dough in half; shape each half into 8-inch long log. Cut each log of dough into 8 pieces. Roll each piece of dough into "snakes". Thicker pieces of dough will make soft sticks and very thin pieces of dough for "grissini" like sticks.

**6.** Lay sticks about 1-inch apart on parchment-lined baking sheet sprinkled with additional cornmeal if desired. Cover; let dough sticks rise until double about 20 minutes.

**7.** Preheat oven to 450 °F. Brush sticks with 1 tablespoon water beaten with 1 egg white; sprinkle with cheese or sesame seeds or coarse salt as desired.

**8.** Bake 3 to 8 minutes or until browned. (Baking time will depend on thickness.) Remove from pan to cooling racks.

**Option:** Omit oil and add 1 cup grated, favorite cheese (Parmesan, Cheddar) to dough.

## Fun Fact:
Wheat and its early relatives were first grown in the Tigris and Euphrates River basin, near Iraq, and became a staple grain more than 10,000 years ago. Egyptians are credited with discovering yeast-leavened breads.

## Family Activity:
Young family members will enjoy shaping "snakes" of bread dough for bread sticks, and brushing (painting) the egg wash on unbaked breads, pastries or other baked goods just before baking to provide a rich color or gloss to the crust.

## Vocabulary:

**Egg wash:**
A thoroughly combined mixture of 1 whole egg, egg yolk or egg white mixed with 1 tablespoon cold water or milk.

**Nutrition Facts (1 serving/42g)**
Calories: 158, Protein: 4g, Carbohydrates: 30g, Dietary Fiber: 1g, Fat: 2g, Mono Fat: 1g, Poly Fat: 1g, Calcium: 6mg, Potassium: 60mg, Sodium: 224mg

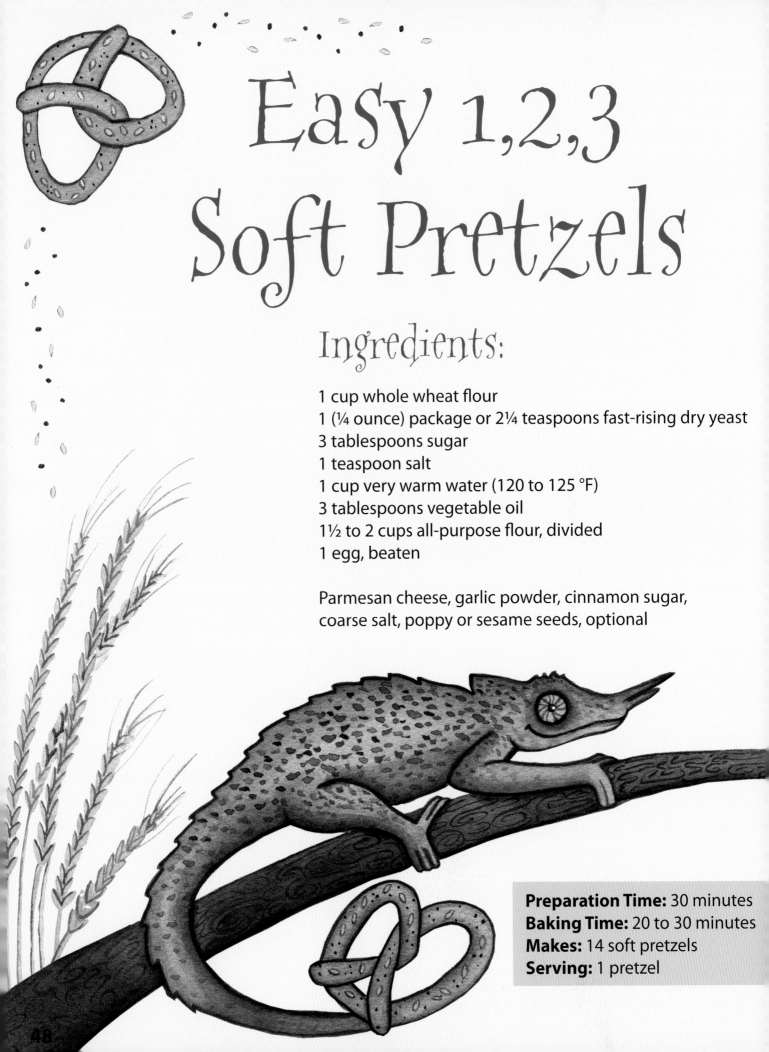

# Easy 1,2,3 Soft Pretzels

## Ingredients:

1 cup whole wheat flour
1 (¼ ounce) package or 2¼ teaspoons fast-rising dry yeast
3 tablespoons sugar
1 teaspoon salt
1 cup very warm water (120 to 125 °F)
3 tablespoons vegetable oil
1½ to 2 cups all-purpose flour, divided
1 egg, beaten

Parmesan cheese, garlic powder, cinnamon sugar, coarse salt, poppy or sesame seeds, optional

**Preparation Time:** 30 minutes
**Baking Time:** 20 to 30 minutes
**Makes:** 14 soft pretzels
**Serving:** 1 pretzel

# Directions:

**1.** Place 1 cup whole wheat flour, yeast, sugar and salt in large gallon-size bag.

**2.** Close the bag. Shake and work the bag with fingers to blend ingredients.

**3.** Open the bag and add very warm water and vegetable oil.

**4.** Reseal the bag and begin mixing by working the bag with your fingers.

**5.** Open the bag and add enough additional all-purpose flour to make a stiff dough.

**6.** Squeeze out the air from the bag and seal the bag with a twist tie near the top. Squeeze and work the dough until the bag pulls away from the dough. If the dough is too dry, sprinkle a tablespoon of water in and keep working.

**7.** Lightly flour hands; remove dough from bag. Place dough on lightly floured surface; knead about 5 minutes until smooth and elastic.

**8.** Cover dough with plastic bag; let rest at room temperature for 10 minutes.

**9.** Divide into 14 equal pieces. Roll each piece into a rope. Cover; let rest 10 minutes until risen slightly and relaxed.

**10.** Roll the rope until it is 20-inches long. Curve ends of each rope to make a circle; cross ends at top. Twist ends once and lay over bottom of circle. Place on greased or parchment-lined baking sheets. Write on the parchment paper to identify who shaped the pretzel.

**11.** Preheat oven to 400 °F. Brush each pretzel with beaten egg and sprinkle with optional topping, if desired. Bake 20 minutes or until golden. Cool on wire rack.

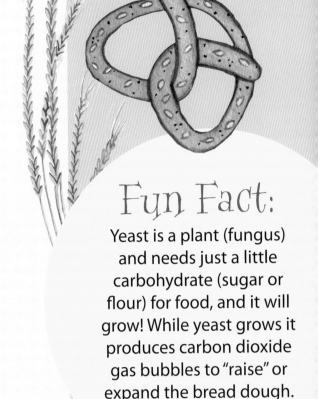

## Fun Fact:

Yeast is a plant (fungus) and needs just a little carbohydrate (sugar or flour) for food, and it will grow! While yeast grows it produces carbon dioxide gas bubbles to "raise" or expand the bread dough.

## Family Activity:

Flatten a piece of dough into 6-inch square or circle; flour lightly, fold in quarters; use kitchen scissors to cut out designs. Unfold and bake on cookie sheets. Cool; sprinkle with powdered sugar.

## Vocabulary:

**Pretzel:**
yeast bread dough originally formed into loose knots by monks and early bakers. Pretzels were shared at weddings as early as 1614 and are a symbol of blessing.

**Nutrition Facts (1 serving/37g)**
Calories: 173, Protein: 4g, Carbohydrates: 23g, Dietary Fiber: 2g, Fat: 4g,
Mono Fat: 1g, Poly Fat: 1g, Cholesterol: 15mg, Calcium: 7mg,
Potassium: 71mg, Sodium: 174mg

# Fruited Focaccia

## Ingredients:

**Dough**

2½ to 3 cups bread flour
   or unbleached all-purpose flour, divided
½ cup whole wheat flour
1 (¼ ounce) package
   or 2¼ teaspoons fast-rising dry yeast
1 cup very warm water (120 °F)
¼ cup sugar or honey
2 tablespoons vegetable oil
1 teaspoon salt
1 cup moistened raisins*
½ cup moistened dried fruit bits*

**Topping Ingredients:**

Egg wash (1 egg beaten with 1 tablespoon milk)
2 tablespoons granulated or coarse sugar

*Cover dried fruit with cold water for 5 minutes and drain.

**Preparation Time:** 75 minutes
**Baking Time:** 15 to 20 minutes
**Makes:** One large loaf, 15 slices
**Serving:** 1 slice

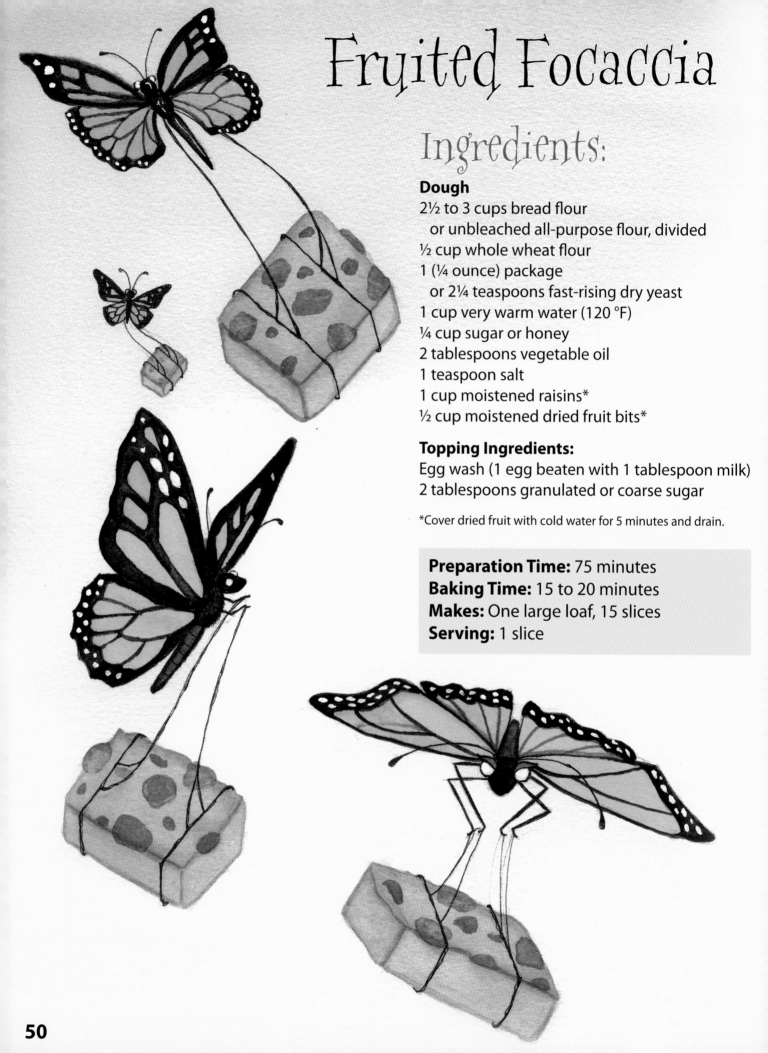

# Directions:

**1.** Combine 1 cup bread flour, ½ cup whole wheat flour and yeast in large mixing bowl.

**2.** Stir in very warm water, sugar, oil and salt.

**3.** Stir in enough remaining bread flour until dough forms a rough ball and pulls away from sides of the bowl.

**4.** Place dough on lightly floured surface; knead about 10 minutes until smooth and elastic.

**5.** Flatten dough, put raisins and fruit in middle and bring edges of dough over the raisins; then knead carefully to mix into dough. The dough will become somewhat stickier as the raisins are kneaded into the dough.

**6.** Place dough into large greased bowl; turn dough; greased-side is up. Cover; let dough rest at room temperature for 10 minutes.

**7.** Grease or line baking sheet with parchment paper. Flatten the dough with hands into a rectangle about 1/2-inch thick and place on prepared pan. Cover with oiled or sprayed plastic wrap.

**8.** Let dough rise at room temperature 45 minutes or until doubled in thickness.

**9.** Dimple the dough by pressing fingertips or thumbs into it, about 1/2-inch deep, 2 inches apart, all over the surface. Let rise until double in size about 30 minutes, at room temperature.

**10.** Preheat oven to 400 degrees. Brush egg wash over the dimpled dough and sprinkle with sugar. Bake 15 to 20 minutes or until golden. Cool on wire racks. Serve warm.

## Fun Fact:

Yeast bread was first baked by the Egyptians, more than 5,000 years ago. They used wild yeast, captured from the air, in starters.

## Family Activity:

For a savory focaccia omit the raisins and fruit. Top the dough before baking with 2 small red or yellow onions, sliced into thin rings and sautéed, 2 tablespoons fresh rosemary or basil, snipped into small pieces, 2 tablespoons olive or vegetable oil and 1 teaspoon salt (may be coarse or kosher salt) if desired.

## Vocabulary:

**Focaccia** was originally baked on a stone hearth and often included fresh grapes during grape harvest. It was considered "fast food" for Italians.

**Nutrition Facts (1 serving/57g)**
Calories: 194, Protein: 5g, Carbohydrates: 38g, Dietary Fiber: 2g, Fat:3g, Mono Fat: 1g, Poly Fat: 1g, Cholesterol: 14mg, Calcium: 16mg, Potassium: 162mg, Sodium: 165mg

# Grandma's Refrigerator Dough

## Ingredients:

½ cup warm water (105 to 110 °F)

2 (¼ ounce) packages
   or 4½ teaspoons active dry yeast

⅛ teaspoon sugar

1½ cups scalded and cooled milk (95 °F)

½ cup butter

½ cup sugar

2½ teaspoons salt

½ cup mashed potato,* squash or pumpkin

2 large or 3 medium eggs

7 cups all-purpose flour (may be part whole
   wheat, as desired)

\* Option - may be leftover or 1 medium
potato cooked and mashed

**Preparation Time:** 50 minutes
**Baking Time:** 10 to 12 minutes
**Makes:** 3 dozen rolls
**Serving:** 1 roll

# Directions:

**1.** Combine warm water and yeast with ⅛ teaspoon sugar in small bowl. Stir and set aside 5 minutes.

**2.** Heat milk in microwave until steaming hot (190 °F). Pour milk into large mixing bowl; add butter, ½ sugar, and salt; mix. Cool to 95 degrees F. or cooler.

**3.** When milk mixture is cooled, stir in dissolved yeast, mashed potatoes and eggs. Gradually add 4 cups flour. Beat at medium speed for 3 to 5 minutes or until smooth. Cover bowl and let dough rest 15 minutes.

**4.** Stir in enough remaining flour until dough forms a ball and pulls away from sides of the bowl.

**5.** Place dough on lightly floured surface; knead about 10 minutes until smooth and elastic.

**6.** Place dough into large greased bowl; turn dough; greased-side up; cover with sealing lid.

**7.** Refrigerate dough, punching dough down after about an hour; reshape dough into a ball, smooth side up. Refrigerate until ready for shaping. Dough will keep in refrigerator one to three days; punch down if needed.

**8.** Preheat oven to 400 °F. Divide dough into thirds and shape each into a smooth ball. Form one dozen rolls from each third of dough. Shape as desired; place on greased baking sheet. Cover; let rise until double in size. Bake 10 to 12 minutes.

# Family Activity:

Make your own pumpkin puree! Wash the outside of pumpkin; scrape inside to remove pulp and seeds. Cut pumpkin in half and place each half cut-side down on baking sheet. Bake at 350 °F. until fork easily pierces pumpkin. Depending on size of pumpkin baking time could be one hour. Cool. Scrape inside of pumpkin to remove pumpkin flesh with spoon and puree in blender.

**Nutrition Facts (1 serving/48g)**
Calories: 136, Protein: 4g, Carbohydrates: 23g, Dietary Fiber: 1g, Fat: 4g, Saturated Fat: 2g, Mono Fat: 1g, Cholesterol: 20mg, Calcium: 18mg, Potassium: 40mg, Sodium: 203mg

# Fun Fact:

Potato, pumpkin, sweet potato and squash are mostly comprised of water (over 75%). Once heated to over the boiling point (212 °F) they cook quickly and become soft and easy to mash. Leftover potatoes and squash are added to bread dough to keep the bread moist.

# Vocabulary:

**Scald:**
to heat almost to boiling. Always be careful when working with hot liquids.

# Monkey Bread

## Ingredients:

2 tablespoons ground cinnamon
½ cup sugar
1 cup coarsely chopped pecans or walnuts, toasted, optional
½ recipe Grandma's Refrigerator Dough (page 52)
1 egg beaten
1 tablespoon water

**Preparation Time:** 30 minutes
**Baking Time:** 30 to 35 minutes
**Makes:** Two loaves, 12 servings per loaf
**Serves:** 24

# Directions:

**1.** Grease two 9-inch bread pans or 12-cup tube pan. Sprinkle bottom of pan with nuts, if desired.

**2.** Combine cinnamon with sugar in small bowl. Divide dough in half. Divide each half into about 24 dough pieces.

**3.** Round out each dough piece; dip in cinnamon sugar mixture. Place tightly against each other in bottom of pan; stack second layer on top as needed. Pan should be about half full.

**4.** Cover; let rise until doubled. Dough will rise to top of pan or slightly higher.

**5.** Preheat oven to 350 °F.

**6.** Combine beaten egg and 1 tablespoon water; brush top of each loaf and sprinkle with remaining cinnamon sugar mixture just before baking.

**7.** Bake 30 to 35 minutes or until top is golden. Remove from oven and place on wire cooling rack. Cool 5 minutes and turn out of pans, upside down. Serve warm.

**Baker's Tip:** Heat a cup of water in a microwave oven. Remove cup. Set pan(s) in a microwave oven; cover loaves with plastic wrap sprayed with pan spray. Close the door. Do not turn oven on. The oven stays warm as the loaves ferment (raise).

## Fun Fact:

Monkey Bread was first called Bubble Bread or Pull-Apart Bread in the 1950's. No one knows for sure why it's "Monkey Bread." Why do YOU think it has this name?

# Family Activity:

Host a party with a monkey theme! After everyone helps make the bread, and while it raises and bakes, choose monkey games—A Barrel of Monkeys, "Tree Tag" (wherever there are nearby trees randomly spaced - choose a base, then everyone starts on a tree - they're safe when they touch a tree). While you eat, read *Caps for Sale* by Esphyr Slobodkina (ages 3-8) and send everyone home with a different colored cap.

## Vocabulary:

**Dough:**
a stiff, pliant mixture of flour, liquid and a few other ingredients (salt, butter/oil, sugar) and usually a leavener such as yeast, baking soda or powder. Dough, unlike batter, is not fluid enough to pour.

**Nutrition Facts (1 serving/48g)**
Calories: 155, Protein: 4g, Carbohydrates: 23g, Dietary Fiber: 1g, Fat: 6g, Saturated Fat: 2g, Mono Fat: 1g, Poly Fat: 2g, Cholesterol: 27mg, Calcium: 26mg, Potassium: 56mg, Sodium: 138mg

# Cinnamon Rolls

## Ingredients:

½ recipe Grandma's Refrigerator Dough (see page 52)
½ cup butter, softened
1 cup packed brown sugar or sugar
2 tablespoons ground cinnamon
1 tablespoon all-purpose flour

**Optional Drizzle:**
1 cup powdered sugar
⅛ teaspoon vanilla
2 tablespoons milk

**Preparation Time:** 15 minutes to shape
**Baking Time:** 18 to 20 minutes
**Makes:** 18 large rolls
**Serving:** 1 roll

# Directions:

**1.** On lightly floured surface roll Grandma's Refrigerated Dough into a rectangle about 24x18-inches and ⅛-inch thick.

**2.** Combine butter, brown sugar or sugar, cinnamon and flour in small mixing bowl; beat on medium speed until smooth and creamy.

**3.** Spread cinnamon mixture over dough leaving about 1-inch of the bottom edge free of spread.

**4.** Moisten edge with water. Roll up jelly roll fashion starting with edge across and farthest from you. End with the edge moistened with water; pinch to seal edge.

**5.** Cut into 18 rolls (1-inch sections) with serrated knife or dental floss. Place rolls on greased baking sheet. Rolls should not be touching.

**6.** Cover with towel or plastic wrap; let rise in warm place (about 90-95 °F) about 30 to 35 minutes or until doubled in size.

**7.** Preheat oven to 375 °F. Bake 18 to 20 minutes or until golden brown. Cool on wire cooling rack.

**8.** Combine drizzle ingredients in small mixing bowl; blend until smooth and frosting will drizzle of the tip of a spoon. If mixture is too thick add a few drops of milk or if too thin ad a little more powdered sugar.

## Fun Fact:

Cinnamon, the bark of a tree, first came from the island of Ceylon (Sri Lanka) and dates back to 2800 B.C. in Chinese writings! With wars waged over it, cinnamon was once so valuable it was fifteen times the value of silver.

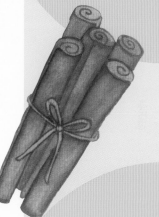

## Family Activity:

Prepare the roll dough one day. The next day enjoy rolling out and preparing the cinnamon rolls. Go for a walk or bike ride while the rolls raise, then pop them in the oven when you get back. Children of any age have fun "drizzling" the fresh cinnamon rolls with icing when cooled.

## Vocabulary:

**Enriched flour:** wheat flour, (such as all-purpose, bread, cake or pastry flour) to which three B-vitamins, iron and folic acid have been added at levels equal to or greater than in whole wheat.

**Nutrition Facts (1 serving/67g)**
Calories: 227, Protein: 4g, Carbohydrates: 35g, Dietary Fiber:1g, Fat: 9g, Saturated Fat: 5g, Mono Fat: 2g, Cholesterol: 38mg, Calcium: 30mg, Potassium: 61mg, Sodium: 221mg

# Pilgrim Bread

## Ingredients:

½ cup water (105 to 110 °F)
2 (¼ ounce) packages
   or 4½ teaspoons active dry yeast
⅛ teaspoon sugar
2 cups boiling water
½ cup cornmeal
¼ cup packed brown sugar
2½ teaspoons salt
½ cup wholegrain rye flour
3 cups whole wheat flour
¼ cup vegetable oil
1 egg
1½ to 2 cups bread flour

**Preparation Time:** 2 hours
**Baking Time:** 35 to 40 minutes
**Makes:** 2 loaves, 16 slices each loaf
**Serving:** 1 slice

# Directions:

**1.** Combine ½ cup water with yeast and ⅛ teaspoon sugar in a small bowl. Stir and set aside.

**2.** Combine boiling water, cornmeal, brown sugar and salt in a large bowl. Let stand for 5 to 10 minutes, cooling to 95 °F or cooler.

**3.** Add yeast, rye flour and whole wheat flour mixture  Beat at medium speed for 3 minutes. Cover,  let stand 15 to 20 minutes.

**4.** Add vegetable oil, egg and 1 cup bread flour.  Beat at medium speed for 3 to 5 minutes or until smooth. Stir in enough remaining bread flour until dough forms a ball and pulls away from sides of the bowl.

**5.** Place dough on lightly floured surface; knead about 10 minutes until smooth and elastic.

**6.** Place dough into large greased bowl; turn dough; greased-side is up. Cover; let  rise until double about 40 minutes. Punch down dough gently and form into smooth topped ball of dough.  Let rest 10 minutes.

**7.** Divide dough in half; shape each half into round or rectangle loaves.  Place round loaves on two greased pie plates or baking sheets, or into greased 8½ x 4½-inch loaf pans.

**8.** Cover and proof in warm (about 85 to 95 °F.) draft free place until loaves are doubled in size and when lightly touched, the small indentation stays.

**9.** Preheat oven to 375 °F.

**10**. Bake loaves 35 to 40 minutes or until golden brown.  Remove bread from pan and cool about 30 minutes on wire cooling racks before slicing or wrapping.

## Fun Fact:

Early colonists prepared their bread dough and baked the loaves in an oven everyone shared.  Wheat was not grown in America – corn was the staple grain raised. When wheat flour was scarce, the colonists substituted some cornmeal to make the wheat flour last longer.

## Family Activity:

Let family members suggest 1½ cups of additional ingredients they would like added to the dough for a "signature" family bread. Add dried fruit, nuts, grated cheese, chopped onion, spices or herbs at the end of the kneading time.

## Vocabulary:

**Gluten:**
two proteins in wheat flour that become stretchy when wheat flour and water are mixed and kneaded.  The gluten in the dough stretches as the yeast creates carbon dioxide, making the bread "expand" or rise.

**Nutrition Facts (1 serving/29g)**
Calories: 107, Protein: 3g, Carbohydrates: 19g, Dietary Fiber: 2g, Fat: 2g, Mono Fat: 1g, Poly Fat: 1g, Cholesterol: 7mg, Calcium: 7mg, Potassium: 86mg, Sodium: 188mg

# Pita Pocket Bread

## Ingredients:

1 cup whole wheat flour
1¾ to 2 cups all-purpose flour, divided
1 (¼ oz.) package or 2¼ teaspoons fast-rising dry yeast
1 tablespoon olive or vegetable oil
1 teaspoon salt
1¼ cups warm water (105 °F)
Cornmeal

**Preparation Time:** 20 minutes
**Baking Time:** 2½ to 3 minute
**Makes:** Twelve 6-inch pita rounds
**Serving:** 1 pita

# Directions:

**1.** Combine whole wheat flour, 1 cup all-purpose flour, yeast, oil and salt in large mixing bowl. Add warm water and stir about 100 strokes or mix 3 minutes on medium speed of electric mixer.

**2.** Stir in enough remaining all-purpose flour to form a ball and dough pulls away from sides of the bowl.

**3.** Place dough on a lightly floured surface; knead about 10 minutes until smooth and elastic.

**4.** Place dough in large greased bowl; turn dough, greased-side is up. Cover with towel or plastic wrap sprayed with pan spray; let rise for 10 minutes.

**5.** Form dough into a long smooth snake shape and divide into 12 equal pieces. Shape the pieces into smooth balls of dough. Cover, let rest 5 to 10 minutes.

**6.** Preheat oven to 475 °F.

**7.** Roll each ball into a flat, round circle about 6 to 8 inches across and ¼ inch thick.

**8.** Place pitas 2 inches apart on ungreased baking sheet pan sprinkled lightly with cornmeal.

**9.** Quickly place pan in lower third of oven so heat is not lost.

**10.** Bake 2½ to 3 minutes or until dough puffs up, surface is dry, bottom slightly browned. Crusts will not get very brown since there is no sugar or milk in this bread. Remove and cool; fill or wrap and freeze immediately. Re-heat oven to 475 °F before baking next pan of pita.

## Fun Fact:

Flat circles of bread take us back in time to the earliest bakers who baked unleavened loaves on hot stones. Bakeries are common throughout the Middle East, but many homemakers prefer to make their own bread and send it out to be baked in the village ovens.

## Vocabulary:

**Yeast:**
fungus that when moist and fed with carbohydrate will grow. As it grows (ferments), it gives off carbon dioxide ($CO_2$).

## Family Activity:

Slice pita bread in half and discover the pocket inside. Fill with favorite sandwich filling for a delicious sandwich.

**Nutrition Facts (1 serving/34g)**
Calories: 127, Protein: 4g, Carbohydrates: 24g, Dietary Fiber: 2g, Fat: 2g, Mono Fat: 1g, Calcium: 7mg, Potassium: 74mg, Sodium: 200mg

# Great Grains Granola

*Granola doesn't require precise measurements and lets families try new ingredients and design their own granola!*

## Ingredients:

3 cups uncooked quick or old-fashioned rolled oats
1 cup rolled wheat or rolled barley*
½ cup wheat bran, oat bran, milled flax seed or wheat germ**
½ cup whole wheat flour
1 cup chopped nuts, sunflower kernels or flaked coconut***
1 cup non-fat dry milk powder
½ cup packed brown sugar or honey
⅓ cup melted butter or vegetable oil
½ teaspoon salt
1½ teaspoons ground cinnamon
1 teaspoon vanilla
1 cup raisins or dried fruit

  * Option:  May use ½ cup rolled wheat and ½ cup rolled barley
 ** Option: May use a combination of wheat bran, oat bran, milled flax seed or wheat germ.
*** Option:  May use chopped nuts, sunflower kernels, coconut or any combination

**Preparation Time:** 15 minutes
**Baking Time:** 25 to 30 minutes
**Makes:** 8 cup
**Serving:** ¼ cup

# Directions:

**1.** Preheat oven 325 °F.

**2.** Combine all ingredients except raisins or dried fruit in large mixing bowl.

**3.** Spread mixture evenly between two ungreased 13x9-inch pans.

**4.** Place both pans in oven. Bake 25 to 30 minutes or until golden brown. Stir every five minutes. (Mixture can also be cooked in a non-stick skillet using medium-low heat.)

**5.** Cool granola thoroughly. Add raisins or dried fruit. Store in a tightly covered container in the refrigerator or a cool dry place.

## Fun Fact:

A whole grain includes all three parts of the grain, endosperm, bran, germ and a wide variety of nutrients. The sum of all three parts contributes important health benefits to every cell of the body.

## Family Activity:

Making granola is a great way to practice measuring skills while expanding your whole grain experience. Measure dry ingredients by spooning dry ingredient into measuring cup and leveling. Measure liquid ingredients with a liquid measuring cup on a flat surface.

## Vocabulary:

**Granola:**
a snack or breakfast cereal made with a variety of grains and rolled oats. Sugar, nuts, seeds and spices are most often added.

**Nutrition Facts (1 serving/59g)**
Calories: 253, Protein: 7g, Carbohydrates: 36g, Dietary Fiber: 5g, Fat: 11g, Saturated Fat: 1g, Mono Fat: 5g, Poly Fat: 4g, Cholesterol: 1mg, Calcium: 80mg, Potassium: 157mg, Sodium: 100mg

# Pet Treats

Bake a special treat for your pet!

## Ingredients:

2½ cups whole wheat flour
½ cup non-fat dry milk powder
1 teaspoon salt
1 teaspoon brown sugar
6 tablespoons cold butter or margarine
1 egg
½ cup cold water

**Preparation Time:** 15 minutes
**Baking Time:** 30 minutes
**Makes:** 10 large or 20 medium pet biscuits

FOR DOGS BIG AND SMALL

# Directions:

**1.** Preheat oven to 350 °F.

**2.** Combine whole wheat flour, dry milk powder, salt and brown sugar in medium mixing bowl. Cut butter into flour mixture using a pastry blender, fork or two knives until mixture resembles coarse crumbs.

**3.** Combine egg and cold water in small mixing bowl.

**4.** Stir the egg mixture into the dry mixture to form a dough ball. Sprinkle with small amounts of water or flour to make a dough that can be kneaded. Knead for about 3 minutes.

**5.** Roll dough to ½-inch thickness. Cut into bone shapes, using cookie cutter or knife. Cut into kibble snacks by rolling the dough into a long thin log, and cut ½-inch pieces. Place on baking sheet. Place the same size on each baking sheet for even browning.

**6.** Bake for about 30 minutes (depending on the size of the pieces) or until browned and crunchy.

## Fun Fact:

Did you know pets can have food allergies? Substitute a blend of non-gluten flours (sorghum, soy, corn) or meal (corn, or flax) for pets with wheat allergies.

## Family Activity:

Make pet treats and donate them to the local animal shelter or include as a specialty gourmet pet treat at a fundraiser bake sale.

## Vocabulary:

**Staple:**
a major product or part of daily life.

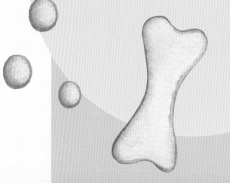

# Rainbow Sugar Chart

For decorating desserts

## Ingredients:

2 cups sugar, divided
Liquid food coloring
6 plastic food storage bags

**Preparation Time:** 15 minutes
**Baking Time:** None
**Makes:** 6 colors, ⅓ cup each

# Directions:

**1.** Place ⅓ cup sugar in each re-sealable plastic bag.

**2.** Use color chart and drop food coloring in each bag to make different colors.

**3.** Remove extra air and seal each bag completely.

**4.** Using hands squish and squeeze the bag to blend color with sugar in each bag.

**5.** Use colored sugar for decorating Quilt Cake, Sugar Cookies, etc.

| COLOR | NUMBER OF DROPS OF LIQUID FOOD COLOR |
|-------|--------------------------------------|
| Orange | 3 drops yellow and 3 drops red |
| Sunset Peach | 4 drops yellow and 1 drop red |
| Yellow | 6 drops yellow |
| Green | 8 drops green |
| Green Apple | 3 drops yellow and 1 drop green |
| Blue | 5 drops blue |
| Aqua | 3 drops blue and 1 drop green |
| Sky Blue | 2 drops blue |
| Purple | 3 drops red and 2 drops blue |
| Red | 10 drops red |
| Rose Petal | 6 drops red and 1 drop blue |
| Baby Pink | 1 drop red |

## Fun Fact:

Primary colors (red, blue yellow) are used to make all other colors. Secondary colors are made when primary colors are mixed (violet, orange, green).

# Family Activity:

Create an edible picture through food decoration. Colored sugars can also be used to roll sugar cookie dough in before baking, to sprinkle on frosted white cupcakes or to create a small "sand" art jar of colored layers.

## Vocabulary:

**Art:**
the conscious production or arrangement of sounds, colors, forms, movements or other elements in a manner that affects the sense of beauty.

# The Thrill of Skill

## Age-Appropriate Kitchen Tasks
*Let older children help teach younger ones –
everyone benefits!*

### 2 years old:
Proper hand washing
Wipe table tops
Play with safe utensils
Scrub, wash, tear, snap, break into pieces
Move pre-measured ingredients from one place
    to another
Add ingredients to a bowl

### 3 years old: *All of the above plus…*
Handle dough, begin kneading, simple shaping
Pour cool liquids into mixture
Mix dry ingredients with wire whisk or spoon in
    extra large bowl
Shake liquids
Spread soft spreads
Place things in trash

### 4 years old: *All of the above plus…*
Peel loose skinned oranges; hard cooked eggs
Form round shapes with dough
Mash fruits (bananas) or cooked vegetables
Cut with dull scissors (snip green onions, dried fruits)
Set table

### 5 to 6 years old: *All of the above plus…*
Help measure dry ingredients (stir, spoon, level)
Cut with a blunt knife (plastic or tableware)
Use a hand held egg beater or whisk
Crush crackers in a bag with a rolling pin
Sprinkle ingredients on salads, cakes, cookies, casseroles

### 6 to 8 years old: *All of the above plus…*
Clean surfaces before and after
Wash fruits and/or vegetables
Gather ingredients and equipment
Grease or spray baking pans
Measure dry ingredients
Measure liquid ingredients
Add measured dry and liquid ingredients into mixing bowl
Learn to crack eggs
Cut fruit, butter or margarine sticks on cutting board
    (plastic or table knife)
Push buttons on blenders, processors with adult
Knead dough
Preheat oven (adults help load products in hot oven)
Wash dishes, put away ingredients or utensils

### 9 to 12 years old: *All of the above plus…*
Learn safe knife skills (chopping, dicing, and cutting)
Handle food equipment safely
Place oven racks and load oven (while oven is cold)
Safe operation of electric equipment (mixer, microwave,
    bread machine food processor, etc.)
Follow a recipe (measure accurately, prepare a product)
Read ingredient and food labels
Safely handle/store ingredients/finished products
Plan and prepare simple meals, snacks
Clean up (how and what to wash in dishwasher or
    by hand)

### 13 years old and up: *All of the above plus…*
Tasks requiring multiple preparation steps or close timing
Create new flavor combinations, shapes or decoration
Plan and prepare whole menus for meals or entertaining
Make shopping lists and shop for ingredients
Help younger children learn about food and how to
    prepare
Enjoy cooking with peers

# Ten Tips for Baking Success

**1. Allow time for family baking.**
- Turn off distractions of television, cell phones and computer.

**2. Wash hands and counter tops before starting.**
- Wear apron or large T-shirt to protect clothes.
- Long hair should be banded or covered.
- Roll-up long sleeves.

**3. Stay safe! See The Thrill of Skill Fact Sheet for age-appropriate baking tasks.**

**4. Before you start: Read the recipe top to bottom.**

**5. Gather all the ingredients and equipment.**

**6. Use the right tools and measure correctly.**
- Pour liquids in a clear liquid measuring cup placed on the countertop and read at eye level.
- Use standard dry measures for dry ingredients.
- Use measuring spoons for small amounts less than ¼ cup.

**7. Ingredient basics.**
- Use butter or hard stick margarine (80% fat), not a spread or reduced-fat product.
- Stir dry ingredients and spoon into dry measuring cups and level with a flat-edged utensil.
- Sift only if the recipe specifies to pre-sift before measuring.
- Avoid measuring ingredients over the mixing bowl.
- Large eggs are the standard used in home baking.

**8. Take it one step at a time.**
- Gather ingredients.
- Do pre-preps for ingredients and equipment as needed.

**9. Oven ins and outs.**
- Before preheating, make sure the oven racks are in the right place for the pans and recipe.
- Allow 10 minutes for oven to preheat.
- Place pans in the oven so they do not touch each other or the oven sides. Do not place pans on racks directly below or above another pan.
- Keep clean, dry oven mitts or pads close by.
- Have cooling racks ready.

**10. Clean up during preparation and while the product bakes.**

# Baking Skills Check List

**What can you do? Check the skills that you already have and get ready to explore and enjoy the wonder of food and the delicious results!**

### Getting Ready

- [ ] Read Recipe Thoroughly
- [ ] Ingredients Available
- [ ] Equipment Available
- [ ] Follow Directions

### Clean-Up

- [ ] Food Safety
- [ ] Clean-up

### Measuring Basics

- [ ] Kitchen Measurements
- [ ] Teaspoons
- [ ] Tablespoons
- [ ] Cups
- [ ] Scales, U.S./English/Metric
- [ ] Dry Ingredients
- [ ] Liquid Ingredients
- [ ] Brown Sugar
- [ ] Shortening and Butter

### Nutrition Information

- [ ] Net Weight
- [ ] Food Label
- [ ] Ingredient Label

### Mixing Methods

- [ ] Muffin Method
- [ ] Biscuit Method
- [ ] Drop Cookie Method
- [ ] Rolled Cookie Method
- [ ] Shaped Cookie Method
- [ ] Cake Method
- [ ] Rapid Mix Yeast Dough Method
- [ ] Straight Dough Method
- [ ] Cool-Rise Method

### Techniques/Terms

- [ ] Shell an egg
- [ ] Separate an egg
- [ ] Sift, blend, whisk
- [ ] Cream
- [ ] Cut-in
- [ ] Knead
- [ ] Ferment, raise, rest, punch
- [ ] Fold-in
- [ ] Peel
- [ ] Slice, dice, grate
- [ ] Roll out
- [ ] Divide dough
- [ ] Simmer
- [ ] Boil

### Equipment

- [ ] Oven Use
- [ ] Microwave Use
- [ ] Hand Mixer
- [ ] Stand Mixer
- [ ] Food Processor
- [ ] Bread Machine
- [ ] Skillet
- [ ] Griddle; waffle iron

## Foods & Nutrition Resources

### Meal Planning

- [ ] Menus
- [ ] Setting a Table
- [ ] Dining Etiquette

### Other:

_____

_____

_____

_____

_____

_____

_____

# Measurement & Ingredient Substitution Guide

**For more baking activities, information on food safety and baking resources go to www.homebaking.org.**

## Measurement Guide

Pinch = 1/16 teaspoon
Dash = 1/8 teaspoon or less
3 teaspoons = 1 tablespoon
2 tablespoons = 1/8 cup or 1 ounce
4 tablespoons = 1/4 cup
5 1/3 tablespoons = 1/3 cup
8 tablespoons = 1/2 cup
16 tablespoons = 1 cup
1 cup = 8 fluid ounces
2 cups = 1 pint = 16 fluid ounces
4 cups = 2 pints = 1 quart = 32 fluid ounces

4 quarts = 1 gallon
1 oz. = 28.35 grams
1 liter = 1.06 quarts

oz. = ounce or ounces
c. = cup
T. = tbsp. = tablespoon
t. = tsp. = teaspoon
g. = gram or grams
lb. = pound

## Ingredient Substitution Guide

1 cup all-purpose flour ............... 1 cup + 2 T. cake flour
1 cup cake flour ........................... 7/8 cup (1 cup - 2 T.) all-purpose flour + 2 T. corn starch
1 package active dry yeast ........... 1 (1/4 oz.) package active dry yeast, 2 1/4 tsp fast-acting yeast
or 1 (1/2 oz.) cake compressed yeast
1 tsp. baking powder ................. 1 tsp. baking soda + 1/2 tsp. cream of tartar
1 cup honey ................................. 1 1/4 cups sugar, or 2 cups powdered sugar + 1/4 cup liquid
1 cup buttermilk or sour milk. ..... 1 T. lemon juice or vinegar plus milk to make 1 cup;
stir and let stand 5 minutes, or 1 cup plain yogurt thinned with milk
1 cup whole milk ......................... 1 cup skim milk + 2 T. melted butter or margarine
1 T. cornstarch ........................... 2 T. all-purpose flour, or 4 tsp. quick cooking tapioca
1 oz. unsweetened chocolate ...... 3 T. unsweetened cocoa plus 1 T. shortening
1 cup packed brown sugar .......... 1 cup white granulated sugar blended with 2 T. molasses
1 large egg ................................... egg whites + 1/2 tsp. vegetable oil, or 1 T. milled flax + 3 T. water,
or 1/4 cup soft tofu (quick breads and cookies only)

71

# Reading List for Baking Literature

| | |
|---|---|
| Designer Oatmeal Cookies | *If you Give A Mouse A Cookie* – Laura Joffe Numeroff |
| Forgotten Chocolate Chip Cookies | *May I Please Have A Cookie?* – Jennifer E. Morris |
| Fudge Brownies | *Beans to Chocolate* – Inez Snyder |
| Apple Dumplings in Cinnamon Sauce | *Up! Up! Up! It's Apple Picking Time* – Jody Fickes Shapiro |
| Country Fruit Cobbler | *Uncle Phil's Diner-* Helena Clare Pittman |
| Gingerbread | *The Gingerbread Girl* – Lisa Campbell Ernst |
| Hot Fudge Pudding Cake | *The Bake Shop Ghost* – Jacqueline K. Ogburn |
| Lazy Daisy Cake | *Fannie in the Kitchen* - Deborah Hopkinson |
| Old-Fashioned Apple Cake Dessert | *Johnny Appleseed* – Jane Kurtz |
| Quilt Patch Cake | *Sam Johnson and the Blue Ribbon Quilt* – Lisa Campbell Ernst |
| Rustic Country Fruit Tart | *Pie in the Sky* – Lois Ehlert |
| Confetti Cornbread | *If You Give A Moose A Muffin* – Laura Numeroff |
| Crispy Whole Grain Waffles | *Everything on a Waffle*– Polly Horvath |
| Flour Tortillas | *If You Lived with the Hopi* – Anna Kamma |
| Katy's  A+ Crepes | *Marven and the Great North Woods* – Kathryn Lasky |
| Pumpkin Pancakes | *Curious George Makes Pancakes* – Margaret and H.A. Roy |
| Basic Whole Wheat Pizza | *A Pizza the Size of the Sun* – Jack Prelutsky |
| Chicken and Dumpling Soup | *The Matzah Man* – Naomi Howland |
| Cheese Quesadillas | *Tomatoes to Ketchup* – Inez Snyder |
| 100% Whole Wheat Bread | *The Spider and the Beehive* – Kama Einhorn (retelling) |
| Bread Sticks | *The Little Red Hen* – J.P. Miller |
| Easy 1, 2, 3 Soft Pretzels | *Walter The Baker* – Eroc Carle |
| Fruited Focaccia | *Yoko* – Rosemary Wells |
| Grandma's Refrigerator Dough | *Pioneer Farm Cooking* – Mary Gunderson |
| Monkey Bread | *Bread, Bread, Bread* – Ann Morris |
| Cinnamon Rolls | *The Sleeping Bread* – Stefan Czernecki and Timothy Rhodes |
| Pilgrim Bread | *If You Lived in Colonial Times* – Ann McGovern |
| Pita Pocket Bread | *Everybody Bakes Bread*– Norah Dooley |
| Great Grains Granola | *The Very Hungry Caterpillar* - Eric Carle |
| Pet Treats | *Dooby Dooby Moo* – Doreen Cronin and Betsy Lewin |
| Rainbow Sugar Chart | *The Story of the Rainbow* - Anne Hope |

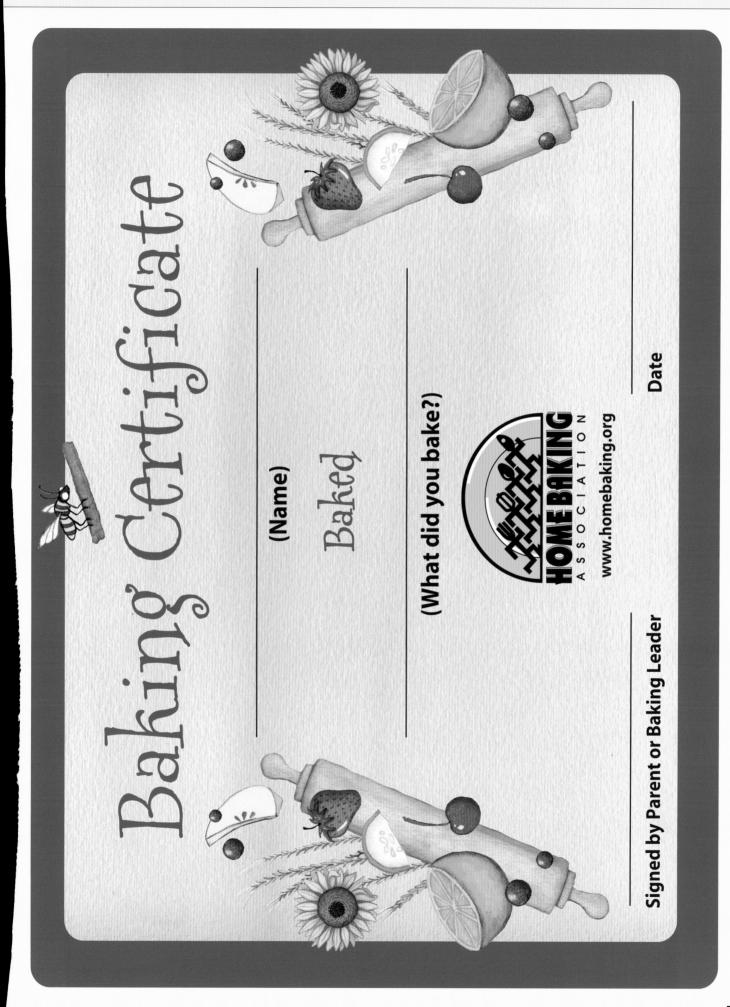

# Baking Certificate

**(Name)**

## Baked

**(What did you bake?)**

HOME BAKING
A S S O C I A T I O N

www.homebaking.org

Signed by Parent or Baking Leader

Date

# Glossary

**Beating**
Making a smooth mixture by whipping or stirring with a wire whisk, spoon, beater or electric mixer to incorporate air into the mixture.

**Blend**
Mixing two or more ingredients together with a spoon, whisk, electric mixer, blender, or food processor just until combined.

**Chop**
Cutting food into small bits.

**Combine**
Mixing together.

**Creaming**
Using a mixer or a large spoon to mix fat (butter, margarine or shortening) and sugar together until creamy and smooth in appearance.

**Cut in**
Blending together fat (shortening or butter) and flour or other ingredients by hand with a pastry blender, two tableware knives or a fork to create a mixture that is crumbly or grainy in appearance.

**Dissolve**
Stirring a dry substance, such as sugar, into a liquid until solids are no longer remaining.

**Dry ingredients**
Refers to the ingredients in a recipe, such as flours, sugar, leavening, salt, baking cocoa, spices or herbs that may be blended before adding to another mixture in the recipe.

**Kneading**
Working dough with the heels of your hands by pressing and folding it and turning the dough a quarter turn after each press and fold. This method develops the gluten, or structure, of the dough.

**Leavening**
Baking soda, baking powder and yeast produce gas in a dough to lighten the texture and increase the volume of baked goods with the production of carbon dioxide. Eggs also are leavening agents.

**Liquid measure**
A clear, hard, plastic or glass cup with a lip for pouring with lines to mark ounces, milliliters and specific measurements. Liquid ingredients should be measured in this cup, with the cup placed on a flat surface for accuracy in measuring.

**Measuring cups and spoons**
Containers or spoons that come in graduated sizes and are used to accurately measure dry or liquid ingredients when cooking or baking.

**Melt**
Heating a solid food such as butter or sugar until it is liquid.

**Mixing**
Stirring, usually with a spoon, until the ingredients are well-combined (no individual ingredients can be seen or identified).

**Preheat**
Heating the empty oven to the recommended temperature before placing the product to be baked in it.

**Proof**
In bread baking, this term indicates the period of time a product is allowed to rise after it is shaped and placed on or in pans.

**Punch down**
In reference to bread dough - when dough has doubled in size or when a dent remains after two fingers are lightly pressed ½ inch into the dough, make a fist and push it into the center of the dough. Pull the edges of the dough to the center and turn the dough over. Cover and let rest or rise again before shaping.

**Spread**
Distributing a product or ingredient in a thin layer over the surface of another product.

**Sprinkle**
Scattering particles of sugar or toppings over a surface, such as a streusel topping for a cake.

**Stir**
Using a spoon to mix ingredients with a circular or figure-eight motion.